Be Kind to Yourself

Be Kind to Yourself

Explorations into Self-Empowerment

GARY NULL

Carroll & Graf Publishers, Inc.
New York

Copyright © 1995 by Gary Null.

First edition 1995.

Carroll & Graf Publishers, Inc.
260 Fifth Avenue
New York, NY 10001

Library of Congress Cataloging-in-Publication Data is available.

ISBN 0-7867-0269-9

Manufactured in the United States of America.

98 97 96 95   5 4 3 2 1

Acknowledgments

I had the good fortune of having the editorial guidance and assistance of a unique and extraordinarily gifted editor, Vicky Koestler. Vicky has managed while maintaining full family obligations and her own professional writing career to also have been of invaluable assistance on this book. She is an editor in the old world tradition of a Sarah Donna or Maxwell Perkins. She offers insightful challenges and constructive and creative input. She also assisted with "Nutrition & the Mind," the life energy books, as well as numerous articles.

My special thanks to her for assisting me along the way.

Contents

Introduction

How can you best be kind to yourself? Although it's a simple question, finding the answer isn't always so simple. It's too important a question to be answered by other people because their solutions may not be right for you. For instance, certain parts of the recovery movement advocate delving into your past in order to understand the traumas and problems that have contributed to your present difficulties in mastering life. But delving into the past is only a tiny beginning step. If you wallow in thoughts of past problems and abuses, and blame others for your present problems, you'll be stuck in your past forever.

So becoming mired in the past and in blame, is not being kind to yourself. You have to go beyond blame if you want to live up to your potential. That's what this book is about—going beyond blame, and beyond the past—and moving squarely into the present to explore how you want to live, and how you can actually empower yourself to reach your own goals.

Many of the sections in this book begin with a question that you can ask yourself as a way of exploring your thoughts and priorities. There are, of course, no right answers. And while I have offered answers of my own throughout the book, you certainly don't have to accept these. In fact, if you question and reject any of my answers, you will be acting in the same ever-questioning, ever-critical spirit in which I wrote this book.

I believe that one should always be asking questions. I remember asking myself some of the most important, and saddest, questions I've ever pondered, on the night of my thirtieth high school reunion. This event is something I keep coming back to in my mind because it made such an impression on me. It wasn't just the fact that most of my former classmates seemed to have physically neglected themselves to such an extent that they now seemed like people who had joined my grandparents' generation. Sure, as a health advocate, that bothered me a lot. But it was much more than that. It was that my former classmates were all so defeated-looking. There was unhappiness in so many of their eyes. And when I asked them about their lives, I heard many unhappy tales—of divorces, tragedies, and, over and over again, alcoholism.

Why?, I asked myself. Why were these people so beaten down by life? Why were so many of their faces unsmiling?

One idea seemed to lighten their expressions. A bright aspect of many of their lives seemed to be the thought of retiring. It was as if after twenty-five years of work they were now nearing the end of a grueling obstacle course, and would soon be able to relax and enjoy collecting their pensions. Yes, retirement in the near future was one thing that my former classmates seemed eager to talk about—retirement and the good times we had had in high school. So those were the highlights for them—the past—school days, and the future—retirement. What was missing was joy in the present.

This is, I believe, a major factor of the problems in our society. We're not taught to value the present. The prevailing belief system tells us to educate ourselves for, to work for, and to generally orient our thinking toward the future. Prevailing belief systems being the powerful forces that they are, this is what we do. What gets lost in the process is the present, and whole lives can go by without the present ever being given its due. That's what I was seeing in those faces at the reunion.

This book, then, is dedicated to our finding fulfillment and success in our lives right now—and to doing so using no one else's notions of success but our own.

By the way, here's my own personal notion of success. It consists of three parts:

1. Knowing who you really are;
2. Spending each day doing what you really should be doing—based upon your knowledge of who you are; and

3. Doing so with joy and love in your heart, so that those you come in contact with feel the effects of your fulfillment.

What's your personal idea of success? In answering this question, it may help to actually write your thoughts down. In any event, as we brainstorm together, please remember the goal.

Be kind to yourself.

Be Kind to Yourself

Getting Rid of Negative Influences in Your Life

GROWTH HAS TO BEGIN SOMEWHERE. START BY EXPLORING BOTH THE constructive and the destructive aspects of your nature. First you must deal with the negative. By dealing with what doesn't work in your life, you're going to know what excuses not to fall back on. You will know why you are not doing the things you dreamed of doing. You will know why you stay with people who don't support and love you. It's a simple matter of deciding which direction you want to put your energies into—positive or negative. Once you understand the consequences of your negative qualities you could say "hold on—do I really want to feel this way or go down this path again? I've been here so many times and I know that what I'm about to say or do or feel is not going to change things. I'd rather choose a positive option when dealing with a negative situation which hopefully would help me resolve this constant repetition of old patterns of behavior. Once deciding I can make a positive change then it merely takes the courage to give it a try.

Breaking destructive patterns is the gateway to getting on with your life. Positive input only becomes significant after you deal with the limiting negative factors. Sure, confronting

3

the negative will make you uncomfortable, but the discomfort is necessary. Change never occurs without it.

Once you understand your negative characteristics, you can claim the real self by saying, "Hold on, I don't buy into this anymore." Once you resolve these issues you will be able to reclaim the dreams of your youth and reenact them as an adult. For every problem, you will be able to find a positive solution.

Do you get unconditional support from your friends and family?

Think about the people in your life. How do you feel about them? Do they care about you? Are they supportive and giving or are they takers? What do they want from you?

Fold a piece of paper in half and record your feelings about each person in a double-entry journal. On one side record your positive responses, on the other side the negative ones. You'll probably have mixed feelings about many people: in these cases write on both sides of the page.

This exercise will help you clarify some of your feelings. You may find that some people expect you to serve their hidden agendas.

Once you define your feelings about these people, you will know which relationships need more nurturing and which ones require more honest communication. If you find there are some people you feel comfortable with part of the time, ask yourself whether the benefits of being with them outweigh the detriments. Are there certain activities you can enjoy together? This will allow you to plan your time accordingly.

Be honest about who supports you and whether that support is conditional or unconditional. Then you will know who is healthy for you.

What are you willing to accept from others?

Be very clear about where you draw the line with others; otherwise, people will overstep your boundaries. Let people know when they are making you feel uncomfortable and that their behavior is unacceptable to you.

One evening last week, for example, someone came to my home unannounced. He said, "I just thought you'd be in," to which I responded, "I'm glad you did. It's good to see you. By the way, I'm so busy lately, you might want to call next time, so you don't waste a trip if I'm not here. It was a thoughtful and polite way to remind him to call first.

If you don't set boundaries you're saying that any area of your life is free and open for people to explore. Then you have no sanctuary. Every human being needs a sanctuary, a place on earth that is exclusively and uniquely his or her own. Sure it's good to be spontaneous at times—to call someone at an unexpected hour—and sometimes it's just plain necessary to do so—but you should always consider people's boundaries and their need for sanctuary as well.

One of the most important sanctuaries is the emotional and intellectual sanctity of yourself. When people say your ideas and feelings are all wrong and start to correct them, they're dishonoring you intellectually and emotionally. That's an emotional assault, a serious offense.

What do you expect from others?

Do people in your life know what you expect from them? Tell them right up front. Either they can meet your expectations or they can't. If they can't, then end the relationship. There's nothing worse than someone saying they can do something when they can't. It creates unrealistic expectations and results in anger and fear of failure.

I look for honesty in my friendships; it's a first priority. I won't allow anyone into my life who lies to me; in fact, I don't believe in second chances once a person has lost my trust. If you give someone a second chance, before long they'll be asking for a third chance, a fourth chance, and a hundredth chance. From what I've seen in my life, I'd say being dishonest is always a pattern of behavior, not just a onetime thing. It's a character flaw that keeps coming up, although sometimes people become clever enough not to be caught.

Unless you tell your friends what you need from them, you'll have ambiguities and contradictions in your relationships. Honest, open communication is essential. If you have trouble expressing your real needs, think about what's holding you back. Are you afraid to lay out your real needs because you worry that no one will honor them? Well, in some cases you're right. They won't. Or can't. But it's better to modify and explain your feelings than to engage in a superficial, meaningless relationship.

Remember, if you're not clear from day one about what you want from a relationship and what someone can give you, much of what you share in that relationship will be built upon false expectations. If it ends, there will be unnecessary blame and recrimination. Who needs that? Just be honest right up front. And be patient. No one can be all things to you or anyone all the time.

Do you stop yourself from attaining basic assets?

Consider the following assets. Do you have negative habits that prevent you from attaining them? You'll find that it helps to actually write these down.

Happiness

Write about the habits you have that keep you from being happy. Perhaps you tend to worry, or you have specific fears. You procrastinate, get angry, suppress your feelings, or compare yourself to others, assuming that other people have something you don't. If only I had their looks, wealth, mate, children, or house, you think, then I'd be happy.

I was running with a man who told me he didn't think we were going very fast. He was comparing our speed to that of some other runners who had just passed us by. I pointed out to him that those guys were bolting at a four-minute pace and must be world-class athletes. We were going at a five-minute pace and doing very well. We weren't as good, but then again, we aren't twenty-two. Don't compare yourself to someone or something you're not.

Health

Write about habits that undermine your health. These might include drinking, being lazy, not exercising enough, thinking negative thoughts, not getting enough sleep, overeating, and worrying.

Fulfillment

What do you do that prevents you from being fulfilled? Look at these possibilities: needing to make a career change, but keeping yourself back; not working up to your potential; never having enough money; procrastinating; being dishonest with yourself; making excuses; having no confidence; lacking focus; not trying for fear of failure; denying yourself the things you want; giving up.

Respect

What do you do that prevents you from being respected? Perhaps you don't respect yourself because your self-esteem is low, you avoid necessary confrontations, you dishonor other people, or you gossip.

I never gossip. If I have something to say, I say it to a person's face. Anyone who talks to you about someone will talk about you. It's a destructive activity that many people engage in. They see someone looking happy, but instead of being happy for that person, they make some kind of snide remark. I won't do that; it dishonors not only the person I'm talking about, but me as well.

Love

What do you do to prevent yourself from being loved? Unless you love yourself, you'll be unable to project love to others and to receive love. You also need to be vulnerable and to be able to take risks. It's difficult to be lovable if you're not open, because no one knows what you're really feeling. When you hold your emotions inside, people can only guess your feelings toward them. Perhaps you're afraid to be honest for fear of rejection, or because you're out of touch with how you really feel.

Financial security

What do you do that prevents you from being financially secure? Perhaps you're afraid to take risks because you're afraid of success.

People who are truly financially secure aren't motivated by money nor are they afraid of losing what they have. People who are afraid of losing money never seem to have enough. No matter how much they have, they continue to work like crazy to acquire more. That shows insecurity. You see this in immigrants who work themselves to death even after they've acquired more than enough money. They never let their children forget how hard they work and how much they suffer. As a result, their children feel guilty about anything their parents give them.

You need to be happy with who you are and what you do. You find security when you adjust your lifestyle so that you're happy with what you're doing regardless of the amount of money attached to it. Of course, you need to accept that your lifestyle is going to be commensurate with what you're doing. For example, if you want to work for charity, your lifestyle will not incorporate fancy cars and lavish furnishings. If you realize that you're getting something else that's more important to you, accepting a simpler lifestyle won't make you unhappy.

When I wrote the first book in this Mastering Life series, *Change Your Life Now,* I didn't seek my regular publisher, Random House. Instead, I chose a publisher with a background in transformational books. My earnings for this book didn't compare to my usual earnings, but the circumstances were different. Random House publishes books on nutrition, but this book was about helping people change their lives. This was particularly important to me because I had just come to understand that people need to learn to change their beliefs before they can change their diets. I'd been doing it wrong for all these years. I'd been writing about nutrition, thinking that people were getting healthier, when they weren't. They needed to change their attitudes first. Then they could change their eating habits. Otherwise, they weren't going to stick to the right diet.

The point is that although I was paid less, I felt that this was the most important book I'd done. I gladly accepted the terms because it was what I needed to do. I'm not measuring my book or my self-esteem by my income. That would be dangerous. I'd start basing decisions on money and end up betraying myself in the process.

How do you control others and how do others control you?

Think of the chase, the capture, and the conquest. After you conquer something or someone, do you begin to lose interest? Look at all the things you thought were important. You put a great deal of time and energy into those projects. Afterward, was what you did no longer important? If so, then control was what you were after.

Or perhaps you've been in this situation. You were the object of someone's affection. As long you were being pursued, the person had an interest in you. But the situation changed as soon as you said, "I'm yours." Suddenly the interest was gone. You were just another trophy. Again, control was the issue.

Do you try to control people? Do you assume that you have the right to? I see this in parents who try to dominate their children instead of respecting them as individuals. Children need to know that they count. Even when children say things that make no sense, a parent needs to respect their right to say them. Too often you hear comments such as, "That's stupid," "You're wrong," "Don't embarrass me." Such remarks teach children to stop being honest. They become afraid of expressing anything, because their parents might judge what they say as being unworthy. They would rather say nothing than risk feeling the pain and discomfort of their parents' rejection.

That starts a pattern of holding back that continues on into adulthood. People refrain from sharing positive, constructive insights. They relate to authority figures as if they were their parents. They follow their boss's dictates unquestioningly as if their own opinion counted for nothing. They search out partners who control everything they do.

When someone controls you, your life is no longer your own. It belongs to someone else. Someone else is building his or her own ego by controlling you. The person never cares about your dreams or treats you as an equal. The person is never there to support you.

Think of how different it would be if you were with people who supported you unconditionally. You'd think, maybe I could really run that marathon, or change my career. Of course sometimes the people in your life *would* really support you if you were honest with them about what you really want to do and be. If you're not honest, you're never going to know.

The people who really care about you for who you are have got to give you the freedom to be who you are. If that means letting go of some control, then they've got to let go of that control. That's why you have to look at who controls you.

Where in your life do you feel empty?

Look, for example, at the following areas of your life:

Empty friend

Are you an empty friend? Here's how I define the empty friend. He or she is the person who always needs something from you. That's the only reason he calls. A "friend" calls and says, "How are you doing, Bob? What's up? It's been three years but it feels like we were just talking yesterday. You're not using that house up on the lake, are you?"

True friends aren't users. They enjoy being with you and they honor who you are. They never criticize or betray you. They defend you when someone else attacks you and they never talk about you behind your back.

If you don't have integrity within a friendship, then what's the point? It's better to let go of that relationship and find another friend. There are no shortages of good people out there. Look for people with good hearts, people who can laugh and who are fun to be with.

Think about the kind of friend you are. Are you able to accept people for who they are? If you can't, you shouldn't be with them. Don't be with someone whom you constantly criticize.

Empty lover

The difference between an empty lover and a real lover is that the latter will always take part of the responsibility for the relationship. The empty lover never does; if something goes wrong, he or she blames you, perhaps calling you a user. When the relationship is working they never complain about your using them.

An empty lover tries to make you feel worthless for wanting to end a relationship that is no longer working. The person doesn't accept that there's a time in a relationship when each person has a right to say good-bye. An empty lover sees the relationship as an investment, and tries to make you feel as if no one else will want you if you end it.

If someone tries to make you feel bad about yourself, just say, "Wrong. I'm not going to feel bad about me." The next time someone tries to put you down, simply refuse to allow that energy in. Then their reality doesn't become yours.

It takes two clashing egos to fight. They can't put you down by telling you how much they enjoyed the time spent together. They're not going to say, "I'm sorry we're not going to spend any more time together but the time we did spend was good." You don't often hear anyone say that, but how much healthier that would be!

Empty patient

Are you an empty patient? I know people who see holistic doctors and then get very angry or disappointed because the doctor is not meeting their needs. They say the doctor gives them too little time or doesn't treat them because they don't have enough money to pay for the treatment they need. Or they say the doctor doesn't believe their symptoms are real. Yes, these may all be legitimate complaints, especially considering that some "holistic" doctors are holistic in self-proclaimed name only.

However, I also see people ignore the insight and advice

their doctor gives them. They never become holistic patients. No treatment ever works for them. They keep going from doctor to doctor.

The empty patient never does anything for himself. When I ask these people why they don't use what they know, they give excuses: "I don't know what to do." "I'm not a doctor." "I don't know what my body needs." Yet they never seem to start educating themselves about what they need to know.

Empty worker

Empty workers resent people who work harder because it shows how little they do by comparison. These people work on automatic. They're at their job just to collect a paycheck. They don't care about what they're doing. They never take responsibility for anything they do and they never give constructive suggestions about how to make the job better.

An awful lot of people in this country are empty workers. I watched people strike at a plant in my hometown. My uncle worked at the plant and I talked to him about it. I said, "You're making a certain income. It's enough to cover your basic needs. I know you want more but there is a price war on with a foreign importer. The importer is subsidized by his government, allowing him to cut prices by twenty-five percent. If your company cuts its price by twenty-five percent it cuts itself out of the business and you're out of a job. Would you rather have a job where you can maintain your standard of living or would you rather go on strike and cause your company to go bankrupt? Then you'll have no job. You will lose your home and a lot more."

I was amazed that these people hadn't thought of that. They were only concerned with having more and milking their company for all they could get. They didn't care about making production more efficient. Six members of my uncle's family were working at a job that required only one person. They were causing their company unnecessary expense. They admitted they could have found other jobs.

Perhaps you've really got to be in business for yourself to appreciate what I'm saying. When you are responsible, you care about making your product or service better and more efficient. Then you're *not* an empty worker, but a caring one.

Starting Now

MOST OF US HAVE SOMETHING IN COMMON: WE GET CAUGHT UP IN our dreams of yesterday. This leads us to think in certainties when practically nothing in our world today is certain. For example, real estate is no longer the investment it once was. In the 1950s you could buy real estate and expect to retire in twenty years. Jobs guaranteed security for life and promised to meet the rise in living expenses. Marriage and relationships used to be more certain too, to the extent that you could often get away with taking people for granted.

When and how do you change?

Positive change won't happen without your input; nothing positive just happens by itself. At some point in your life someone has probably told you that things will get better. Think about what that means. Do things get better on their own? If you don't actively construct a program that allows you to move from one place to another, you'll never reach your goal. You must have a program and you must be the architect of that program. No one else can make changes for you. You can have support from other people, but making the change is your responsibility.

Change usually happens over a period of time, not all at once. When I help people train for a marathon, I teach new skills in increments. Only when the new runner has mastered one portion of the training do we take them forward. Otherwise they will burn out.

Compare your journey of self-appreciation to the old tradi-

15

tion of apprenticeship. An apprenticeship can take years and years. You can't expect to instantaneously get in touch with your real self at a weekend workshop.

When should you start making a change? My suggestion is right now. Making preventive changes in your diet and lifestyle, for instance, is better than waiting until after the diagnosis of a disease. Then you have some life-threatening problem to face and are more likely to respond out of fear, and to follow some outside authority's dictates of what is right for you, rather than your own inner motivation.

Are you changing to please others?

Most people look for direction outside of themselves and neglect to look within. Right now there are over five million Americans involved in cult practices. Most are not in Moonie groups or something that obvious. Rather, people embrace things that on the outside seem reasonable—The One Heart Movement, The One Mind Movement, The One World Movement. But ultimately these are still cult practices. They preach about how life really is and how it should be. They point out all the things in your life that don't work and show you that by doing things their way, everything in your life will work. People who engage in such practices are giving someone else the responsibility of making their lives work and are ultimately disempowering themselves.

You will never be able to sustain changes that another person makes for you. All you will do is be obedient to that other person's program. You will be eating certain foods, chanting, meditating, doing service in the community to show that authority figure what a good, obedient person you are. Finally you will have changed by discarding all the features that make you unique. You will no longer be you. You'll have become the person that the authority figure won't get angry with.

Ultimately, change, to be meaningful and sustainable, must come from within. When you do something, ask yourself whether you're doing it because you want to. Are you honoring something inside? Or are you doing it to be recognized by some father figure, mother figure, or religious figure who is validating your existence?

In what ways do we disguise our real self?

Do you disguise your true nature? Why hide something that's naturally you? Are you insecure or ashamed about who you really are? Are you afraid of rejection? Do you feel inadequate?

Our society makes us feel as though we must achieve something in order to be acceptable. You feel that you are not acceptable just as you are. You try to react to everything people say. You think if you don't conform, people are not going to like you. I'd better give them what they want, you think. There's less hassle. After all, you get rewarded if you give them what they want, and you get punished if you don't. The problem is, without honesty there is nothing natural in what you're doing or how you're feeling. Your life is then based upon the artificial, and the artificial has no bottom, no base.

When you're dishonest in your work, you will overcompensate and try to get the emotion you want from your friends and family. But that doesn't work. You're still in a bottomless pit. You can't be one thing to one person and something else to another. When we project different images to different people it can create enormous confusion.

Being honest makes you vulnerable. Conversely, only when you are vulnerable are you honest. When you are vulnerable, you're open. When you're open you're expressing what is natural with a sense of self-balance. In other words, you're acknowledging who you are. You're sharing true intimacy.

Intimacy means you're expressing what you really feel. You're laying it out. A person can accept or reject it. But they must also respect that you have a sanctity within which you alone make the decisions. You alone decide who comes into your sanctuary and shares the self. And if others are going to share the self, you make sure that they share the self as you have expressed it, not as they would manipulate it. The result is that you have allowed yourself to be vulnerable without changing what you're being vulnerable about in order to meet the needs of other people.

That's the desired result, anyway. What sometimes happens is that when someone knows you're being vulnerable and open and honest, they take advantage. They try changing you. You have given them access; you've said, here's what I am. Here's what I feel. But then they say, oh good; now let me set you straight. Suddenly we realize, hold on, that's offensive.

And it is. No one should offend you when you have opened yourself up to them. You have the right to say, "I shared my real inner self with you. If it's not good enough as it is, I'll have to say good-bye."

If you don't resolve this issue—either feel completely comfortable or walk away from the situation—you're going to be hurt.

Vulnerability allows you to be as free and flexible as possible. It gives you movement, fluidity, a full range of intellectual and creative expression.

Without vulnerability you are closed, rigid, fearful of being discovered for your inner passions. When you're not vulnerable you can't move. You're stuck. You get stuck in a job, stuck in a relationship, stuck in a career, stuck in a place. You may try to defend the merits of being stuck rather than open yourself up to move on. You may spend more time defending the ego than you do in realizing that there is nothing to defend in being open.

You never have to defend vulnerability. You never have to defend the true and honest self.

Compassion, sensitivity, and openness come when a person feels comfortable with who he or she is, and when he is willing to give the quality of that energy to another human being. But, remember—it serves no purpose to give the quality of your inner being to people who either abuse it or deny its virtue. Give your gift to one of the many deserving people in this world who would honor that gift and do something positive with it.

To know yourself requires knowing what you're not. I think it's very important that you determine what you are not! Frequently to understand what you are is to acknowledge what you are not.

For instance, if I am not a liar then I'm honest. If I'm not a thief, then I can be trusted. You might find it helpful to make an entry in your journal for each thing that you are not. It then becomes easy to generate a list of what you are.

When you remove your masks, whom do you see?

Everyone has a mask. Some people wear many. They spend their lives perfecting their images. Most people want to look a certain way, talk a certain way, be a certain way, cultivate a certain presentability and a certain acceptability. Usually the image is not the inner person but altogether different.

Why do we do this? Perhaps it's because as children, we learn to act a certain way in order to be accepted. At home we adapt to our parents' needs and in school we work to please our teachers. For every positive lesson, twenty more are negative and limiting. We learn that we are not smart, not right, not good, and that we will be punished for being ourselves. We change to appease the adult world. It's a survival mechanism.

Then one day, many years have passed, and we've forgotten who we really are. The mask becomes like a virus in a cell; it thinks it is part of us. So how do you change this situation?

Begin by looking at what doesn't feel right. Ask yourself whether you are wearing a mask to hide an essential part of you. Only during the process of being honest and open can you begin to change. You can begin to see who you really are beneath the mask.

Write about the masks you wear in life. Is there a particular one that you usually wear? What is it meant to protect? Remove the mask and listen to the person underneath. What do you hear? Do you hear the same perspective or a different one? Are you an obedient person or a challenging one? A dynamic person or a passive one? Do you hear a person who wants to join something, or a person who wants to lead the way?

Asking yourself the next question will help you explore some of the reasons you might mask your feelings.

What causes you discomfort?

Many things in your life can cause discomfort. These are just a few to consider.

Change

Change takes you to unfamiliar territory, and that can be unpredictable and scary. When you're in a new situation there are no guidelines to follow and you don't know what will happen next. Your old masks may not work for you there.

Change is a necessary prerequisite for growth. But most people will only allow change into their life when they are so dissatisfied with their circumstances that they can no longer bear life as it is. Seldom do people change just to try something new and different. That means that some things in your life will change, but an awful lot won't. And often, it's what you don't change that is counterproductive to your growth.

Stress

You need not fear stress. Stress-provoking situations can be used to your advantage. You can challenge yourself and become stronger for facing stress. Ignoring it, on the other hand, will only cause you more *distress* and make you weaker. When I get into a cab that's not air-conditioned on a hot summer's day, I have a choice. I can either worry about becoming clammy and sticky or I can relax, roll down the window, and enjoy the breeze hitting my face. You have choices as to how you will handle a stressful situation.

Most stress comes from inappropriate reactions. You can keep from becoming stressed by getting into the habit of watching yourself for overreaction. If your accountant says you owe this or that tax, you can blow up at her as if it's her fault or you can simply deal with the situation. When I get audited, the first thing I say to the accountant is, "Worst-case scenario, how much will I owe?" Then I write out a check and say, "If it turns out that I don't have to pay that amount, you'll return the balance." I go on with life. After all, it's only a piece of paper. It's nothing until I make it into something.

Telling the truth

Telling the truth can be uncomfortable. It can startle people because they're not used to hearing it, and it puts you in the position of dealing with their reactions. Therefore, upon reflection, you may find that you're rarely, if ever, completely honest with anyone.

Start being honest, in a sensitive way with no intention of hurting anyone, and just expressing what's inside. Right away people will know where you stand. It's better, I feel, to be right up front with people so that they can accept or reject you based upon who you really are. Otherwise, you're playing the game of trying to get acceptance for what you don't really mean.

Make a list of values that are important to you. Be honest about what they are, how you feel, what you want, the real you.

Recall situations in which you have been dishonest with someone. Ask yourself the reason. Did you want the person's approval? Know that your happiness does not depend upon another person's accepting you. Know too that you are really doing yourself a disservice by lying to people.

You can say anything when it is in the spirit of love. Not only will you help others that way, you will be true to yourself as well.

Failure

When you experience a failure, what do you see and how do you feel? Failure can be perceived positively or negatively.

When you experience a failure you may interpret it as you being a failure. You may equate what you accomplish with who you are. Failing, then, becomes a judgment against your self-esteem, an affront to your ego. This misperception goes back to childhood, when you were made to feel uncomfortable or unacceptable for doing something wrong. Perhaps your parents reprimanded you for getting a C on your report card when your brother got an A. Suddenly, you were no longer good enough just as you were. You felt you had to succeed to be loved and accepted.

Ironically, once you're in this mindset, no matter how successful you become you never feel that you're good enough. Look at the actions of businesspeople dealing in millions and billions of dollars who never find contentment no matter how much money they have. They play with other people's money, caring only about how much they can profit themselves. Look at what we went through in the eighties, when billions of dollars were made and lost and lives were devastated. According to an article in *Spectrum* magazine, five million lives were displaced in the 1980s by leverage takeover buys. Even middle-class Americans who didn't play a part in the game were harmed in the process. Think of the legacy left by these Wall Street manipulators. We haven't even felt the full effects of it yet. How many of those people were living with a fear of failure?

Fear of failure can stop you from trying again. A lot of people never try to do anything a second time because the first time they tried it, it didn't work. Failure to them becomes a way of justifying that they should never have tried in the first place. It then justifies what they suspected all along: "Gee, I can't be a writer." "I can't run a marathon." "I can't work in another career." That attitude keeps people in the same old predicaments.

And it's not a realistic attitude. Hardly anyone does a thing right the first time. Most people do things consistently wrong, repeatedly failing for a long time before they succeed. When you look at Fred Astaire flawlessly dancing, what you see is the finished, edited product of a year's effort to make a film. What you don't see are all the mistakes in the hundreds of outtakes that led up to that point of perfection. Likewise, when you see a martial artist demonstrating tai chi or karate, you don't see all the practice it took to get that person to his or her level of mastery.

The best way to perceive failure is as something that didn't work. This just means that you need to do something different the next time. Then, failure never becomes something that limits you or takes you to a dead end. It becomes something that strengthens you, helping you to see what doesn't work. This is a healthy way of looking at failure.

Be willing to learn from your errors. Learn like a child learns. Children fall down, get back up, and try again. They don't expect to walk the first time they try. They don't let their falling affect their self-esteem. That's an attitude adults should adopt as well.

Fear

Most fears are the result of imagination. You imagine a situation, worrying about what might happen *if.* . . . You think, "I would change my job, but what if I don't find another one, or what if I do find another one and it doesn't work out?" You start seeing all the negative possibilities instead of the positive ones.

Unfortunately, many people don't know how to respond positively to fear. They may develop obsessions for anything from food and alcohol to sex. They may blame their problems on the lack of a loving relationship. They may think, if only I had someone to love, everything else in my life would fall into place. People have many ways of disempowering themselves in the face of fear, rather than confronting what's bothering them.

The only way to deal with fear is to face it. Once you confront what you are afraid of, you can start looking at all possibilities and preparing yourself for change. You can focus on gathering the tools you need to get the job done. The fear often vanishes in the process.

Name one thing you would like to change in your life but feel fearful about confronting. How do you circumvent the issue? List the negative and positive consequences of changing. Then list what you can do to minimize the negative and prepare for the change you want. Repeat this exercise every week. At the end of the year you will have changed ten to twenty negatives into positives.

Loneliness

When you feel lonely, you generally feel sorry for yourself. Sometimes you're just a victim of the unquestioned assumption that aloneness equals loneliness, when in fact aloneness can be a wonderful opportunity for introspection and growth. Sometimes you decide that you can't feel lonely if you belong, so you might become a joiner to evade feelings of isolation. Joining something is not necessarily a bad thing to do, but you have to look at your reasons for doing it. Are you joining a group only because you don't have a life without it? Or are you bringing something positive to what you do?

There are other areas to explore when you're looking at sources of discomfort; these include feelings of guilt, pain, and disappointment.

What limiting patterns do you engage in?

Do an honest self-evaluation. Each week look at one area of your life to see if you can improve it. Notice any habits that limit your ability to grow, perceive, communicate, share, feel, and be honest with yourself and others. For instance, do you keep your appointments, or do you tend to break them? Do you organize your day to get in what you want to do, or do you just meander through the day? Do you overorganize? One way to never get anything done is to overplan. We do not appreciate that constant planning can take us away from the process of change. Some people constantly plan for what never gets accomplished; all they do is engage in the procrastination game.

Another important question to ask yourself: Do you have the patience to listen to others with care, or are you always simply waiting for them to shut up so you can talk?

List the patterns that you perceive as being self-limiting. Then work on changing them. By doing that, you will be able to grow.

Being wrong

How do you know what's wrong? Is your idea of wrong based upon what someone taught you? And do you find that much of what you were taught is accurate based on your own experience?

Look at sexism. How much male behavior is based on the conditioned belief that women are sexual objects for conquest? I would say most of it; it's a big part of human male behavior. Yet we know it is wrong to use someone purely as a sexual object and not to see her as a human being.

On the other side of the coin, many women are taught that they are nothing without men and that their primary goal should be to make themselves indispensable to men, doing things for a man that he could easily do for himself. This is common behavior, and it's disempowering behavior, to say the least.

Most people are trained to be obedient and never challenge authority. Even when they see a gross injustice they learn to keep their mouths shut. Everybody in our society, with some rare exceptions, is taught to obey authority. Is that a behavior to be questioned? Is it wrong to speak out against authority when you see injustices done?

And what about education? How many curricula in this country are designed to help a child explore his or her own needs in a constructive way? On the contrary, students are conditioned to passively accept what they are being taught and never challenge the instructor. Is it wrong to have your own ideas when they disagree with the teacher's? Is it wrong for a teacher to teach a curriculum that differs from the course his superiors have set? Whom do you threaten when you want to grow beyond some of the limitations, biases, and prejudices in the educational structure? When I was in school studying nutrition, repeatedly I tried to question the teachers when they said sugar was good. It wasn't long before I was told that I would be thrown out of class if I opened my mouth again.

Explore your own beliefs of right and wrong. Do your beliefs disempower you and others? If so, look at where those beliefs come from and begin to challenge them.

Feeling inadequate

What in your past leads you to believe that you or other people are inadequate? Particularly, what role does society play in contributing to that notion? Let me give you an example. In this country fewer Native American children go on to higher education than in any other demographic group. Yet, when is the last time you heard anything about the problems of the Native Americans and their educational system?

The fact is that our war against Native Americans has continued into this century. In this century, Native American children were not only forced to learn English; they were actively discouraged from engaging in their own cultural practices. They were not even allowed to practice their native rituals. When they would start their rituals, helicopters from the American Forestry Service and the Bureau of Indian Affairs would come in and disrupt them. Their practices were considered heathen.

Native Americans couldn't own land off the reservations— which was a good way of keeping them there. Long after everyone else had the right to vote, the Native American did not.

The myth still perpetuates. I know of a Native American woman who auditioned for a role in a movie. Although she was educated and intelligent, she was asked to act as if she were stupid. She didn't fit the image people had of Indians, she was told. The woman refused to act dumb just to fit a stereotype.

Other cultures are also excluded from power and made to feel inferior. Have we ever had a Hispanic Supreme Court justice? How often do you see Hispanics featured in major motion pictures or in a television series in a real-life situation? Usually Hispanics are portrayed as pimps or gang members. You see only the worst stereotype, and by portraying only this biased picture we make a group feel inadequate.

Another way people are made to feel inadequate is through age discrimination. (This is especially true for women. Often in our society, women over thirty or forty stop revealing their age because they are afraid of being judged for it.) Older people have been made to feel inadequate and no longer an essential part of society. We try to dispose of them instead of seeking out their intellectual and emotional wisdom and learning from their lifetimes of experience. Sadly, excluding our aging population is a loss to everyone, young and old.

But then, such losses are inevitable considering our society's superficial point of view. We notice a person's looks, build, age. What happens when a person doesn't have those things anymore? Is he or she suddenly less of a person? We set standards for perfection that nobody can meet.

You can have wonderful relationships with people of any age if they are based on equality. Some of my best friends are people in their eighties and nineties. I became friends with them when they were in their seventies and eighties. And what did I share with them? Everything. I didn't focus on our differences; I looked at what we could share equally.

Being judgmental

Being judgmental is a way of defending your self-esteem, because if you put people down, you feel better about yourself. But this is a terrible way of feeling good about yourself.

What if people are being unfairly judgmental about you? I find it's best to choose a loving reaction. I can take a step back and say, "You don't like me? That's alright. You don't know me. If the time ever comes when you want to know me, maybe you'll think differently. But you can go ahead and have your feelings. I'm not going to have any anger in return." That kind of response is going to make a person think.

Obsessing

You obsess when you become constantly preoccupied with unresolved conflicts. For example, you are spurned by a loved one. You feel rejected because someone you love will not reciprocate. This causes you to become preoccupied with thoughts about why the person is not returning your love. What's wrong with the person for not seeing how wonderful you are? Or what's wrong with you that is making you unacceptable to that person?

You must accept that if someone does not want you in his or her life, that's the person's choice. You need to move on. There is no shortage of nice people who will enjoy and accept you for who you are without all the extra effort.

Obsessive behavior is obviously unhealthy. Once you become obsessed, it's hard to see anything from a balanced perspective. When you see yourself obsessing over someone or something, you should seek professional help.

Blaming

Many people find it easier to blame than to think. What if you don't blame but just accept certain things being the way they are? For example, if you're a parent of a teenager who doesn't keep his room neat, plays loud music, rushes through meals, and leaves dirty clothes all over the place, your first response might be, "What's wrong with this person?"

But perhaps it would be better to stop and think, is it possible this person's perceptions, though different from mine, are justified? Maybe he is at a time in life when it's okay to be messy and disorganized and to have multiple interests all competing for his attention. Maybe it's alright for your teenaged daughter to be inconsiderate toward others in her immediate environment. This is generally something people grow out of once they become responsible for themselves and others.

Consider the behavior of the person you are blaming. Is their behavior really the issue or are you making it an issue to avoid dealing with your own pain?

Are you the kind of blamer who tends to criticize virtually everything and never feels good about anything? For example, you go away to a resort in the middle of winter, where you have the opportunity to sit in the sun and relax for a few days. Instead, you're concerned about the size of your room or the waiter who gave you poor service. You blame someone or something for your inability to relax and be happy. You take your pattern of blaming with you wherever you go. No matter how good something is, you find a way to make it less enjoyable.

Are you the kind of blamer who blows everything out of proportion? For example, you're a homemaker who cleans so much that the moment someone comes in and makes even the slightest mess, your day is ruined.

If you are a blamer, you should seek help to understand the cause of your blaming. You should also try to get some feedback from the people you've been accusing about how they see you. Usually these people will keep their thoughts to themselves because you like to be in control and to have the final word. But if you are open to feedback and ask for help, people will generally offer you an honest picture of yourself. Then you will start to see how your actions affect others. This is not to assume that you should see yourself only as others see you; rather, you should use it as a reference point, keeping in mind that everyone's perceptions are different. Your sense of humor, funny to you, may seem cruel and insensitive to others. The question is—is it cruel or were you simply looking at something from a different perspective? Clearly, we cannot please everyone, but it would be wise to be aware of how others perceive you so that you can modify your actions and be more sensitive. This does not mean that your jokes are not funny—but they might not be funny to everybody.

Begin your own twelve-step program

You must take action to actually start improving your life. After examining old patterns of behavior that limit you, you can take steps to obliterate those patterns by adding one new thing to your life each month. You create your own one-year, twelve-step program. (Of course you can work faster or slower as needed, and you can tailor the program to meet your needs. The key is to start by assessing what you need to make your life work.)

Gradually change all areas of your life. Don't trick yourself by changing only one aspect. That's creating imbalance; a perfect example of this is when a person works nonstop at his or her career but neglects other important areas of life, such as personal relationships. People who do this are still looking for approval and not dealing with real needs in a way that will ultimately lead to greater happiness for themselves as human beings.

Here are some steps you can take to become more whole. There are twelve of them, in keeping with the idea of a twelve-step program.

Include sacrifice and service in your life

This comes from within. What do you give back to the world? You cannot serve others if you think the world is there just for your taking. John Wayne said in a 1971 interview that he believed we were fair with the Indians. They weren't using the land so we took it to make use of it. The underlying premise was basically that if one group is stronger, smarter, and wealthier than another, it's okay for them to take the other's land, assume ownership, and displace the other group from their homes. That mentality is the opposite of service and sacrifice.

For me Rachel Carson exemplifies the idea of sacrifice and service. She said back in 1960 that we can't keep abusing the environment without repercussions. She cautioned us about the finite amount of abuse that anything can take; she took a lot of abuse herself for performing the great service to mankind of warning us about DDT, our disappearing bird life, and our responsibility to the planet. Sacrifice and service take great courage in our society.

Every movement in this country starts with one person's efforts. One individual can make a great difference. Ask yourself what difference you can make. What do you have to offer? Become an expert in one area and share what you've learned. Your life can be an example to others.

Set your goals—then get going

Once you've set a goal for yourself, don't let apprehension impede your progress. Your negative expectations can overwhelm you. It's never good to concentrate on your problems; focus instead on what you want to achieve.

When I've got to get a job done, whether it's making a documentary, writing a book, or presenting a workshop, I don't let my expectations of the project limit me. If I started thinking that I needed to come up with $300,000 before I can make a documentary, and worrying about finding a camera crew and getting it on the air, I'd never make it happen. Similarly, if you want to write a book but spend all your free moments worrying about finding time to write, you'll never get it done.

Instead I forego any expectations I might have and simply

start to make my documentary or write my book. When selecting a documentary to produce, I try to find one that will be relevant to the most people. For example, with one like "A More Natural Approach to Treating and Preventing Cancer," it may take me a year of research before I begin filming—I have to interview patients who have been successfully treated, doctors who have gone beyond the limitations of the orthodox treatments, and therapists such as herbalists and homeopaths who play an essential role in prevention and treatment. But during every step in the process I continue to reshape and remodel what will become the final product. In the interim I send out letters explaining the documentary as if it were complete to see which noncommercial stations in the United States would find it of interest. By the time filming is completed I know how many will air it, and which video rental and sales catalogs we will offer to the public. It's not a difficult process.

Evaluate the possibilities for your new self every day

When you get up in the morning and look at yourself in the mirror, be happy with what you see. Know that you are growing and learning. Be pleased with the progress you've already made.

Then do something different. Every single day do at least one new thing. Say something positive and encouraging to someone you meet. Dress or cook in a novel way. It can be anything. The important thing is to change something each day.

Relinquish an old pattern

Give up one pattern of behavior that no longer serves you such as always talking over someone, never allowing them to finish a statement—it shows disrespect for the person as well as lack of interest in what they're saying. Instead try to listen fully to what someone says before responding. When you see that pattern emerging, don't allow it back into your life. Do something more constructive instead. Reaffirm the new behavior, which will in time become a new pattern that helps your life work.

Create or join support teams

Anytime you need help in your life you can find people willing to support you. Many fine people in this country have gone through crises, have survived them, and are now stronger for it. Sharing what they've been through helps you and strengthens them as well.

Have a daily conversation with your old and new selves and write a headline

This is an activity I engage in each evening for a half hour before going to bed. First I consider how I would have lived that day if I were not growing. Then I look at the way I actually handled my day. I write a headline for myself, based upon my day. Today, for example, I went out of my way to help a senior citizen. I went to a soup kitchen and spent an hour helping to serve meals to homeless individuals. I helped the environment by cutting out a couple of articles from an environmental magazine, making 50 copies, and distributing them through my office in the hopes of raising the consciousness of others. And I honored my body by only feeding it good, healthy food.

As the architect of your day, what would you like to say about what happened? Perhaps you will write something like, "I forgave my parents today for the abuses of a lifetime." Once you write a headline, you reaffirm the new way you are living. This helps you continue the process of change.

Write a different headline for each day. At the end of a year you'll have 365 headlines describing how you changed your life.

Burn the negative bridges behind you

The symbolism behind the idea of burning bridges is that you acknowledge your movement from a comfort zone. You are allowing yourself to move forward and get on with your life.

When you resist the idea of moving ahead you choose to recross the same old bridges. It seems simpler because you know the outcome. People respond to you in a familiar fashion and you get your way.

Although it seems easier on the surface, that approach to life has serious shortcomings. If you follow the old patterns of behavior, you stay stuck in the same old problems. You turn to food, drugs, or alcohol as an outlet or to negative people for advice. You repeat destructive actions.

Once you realize that you can't get back in a door that's closed forever, you reaffirm life every day. You don't devote time and attention to old patterns of thinking and behaving. Instead of feeling frustrated and blaming yourself and others for your life's failings, you now recognize that this is a different day and you need to live a different way. The only way to do that is to realize that yesterday's bridge is burnt and to affirm that today you are waking up with a new focus that is going to make the day productive and positive.

Then you simply disallow that the old bridge is useful. You turn away from the old system and choose to honor life instead. Even if it's rough, you're going to leave your comfort zone and feel the discomfort of uncertainty. You're going to stretch your mind, body, and spirit to learn new patterns of behavior, new ways of relating, new ways of listening, and new ways of doing things. You're going to go over a new bridge.

Realize that reality is better than fantasy

Most people dream of doing things but never actually do them. They may make an attempt to start something new but stop themselves short of actualizing it. They dream about finding a new job or starting their own business, but never do anything about it. They remain where they are and continue to live in frustration. Perhaps their work environment is very toxic and they're breathing in unhealthy chemicals. Maybe their job provides no challenge or fulfillment. Instead of changing that, they just fantasize about working someplace else.

Maybe they're in a relationship that is more harmful than supportive. Although they're unhappy, they do nothing to change their situation. They fantasize about ideal relationships with people they've never met, even when making love.

At some point you need to say, "It's my life, let me live it. Let me be honest about what I need to make my life more fulfilling." That's the hard first step, but it's worth it because when you actually start making changes, those changes can be so profound and exhilarating!

Keep everything in perspective

Don't blow things out of proportion. Question your perceptions of the world and know there are other ways of looking at things. If you want a really humbling experience, spend some time on an Indian reservation. See people who are trying to survive with almost nothing, who are still trying to find life and meaning in the midst of almost total deprivation.

Look at our own culture's values and compare them to those of the Indians and other cultures around the globe that value Mother Earth. We dishonor the earth and use it to serve our needs without giving back to it, but not all cultures approach life that way. The Indians lived making only imperceptible changes to their environment, while we have radically changed the earth. We assumed we had the right because we had the might.

Question what you see, and know that there are different ways of viewing the world. Then you're not in conflict with others and you can pull back and see life in a larger perspective. Things won't get blown out of proportion. Have you ever wondered how the world would be different if you had never been born? What difference have you made? Native Americans realized that there was a deeper meaning and purpose to life. That, in turn, shaped their perception. They never killed more buffalo than they needed to eat and to clothe themselves. They would not deforest an area just to have a better view. The idea of random exploitation of people or environments was alien to them. In our culture, however, many people are trying to assess the significance of their lives. Everyone has something to share that's positive and meaningful and lasting. Think of the doctors who know they've saved lives. The draftspersons who, because of their labor and ideals and pride in their work, have created products and services that have allowed untold numbers of people to enjoy a better and safer quality of life. When you begin to look at all the conflicts we engage in, ask "Could I change my perceptions to see this conflict from a different perspective? Would it change my response as well as the outcome?" By doing this, we see that so much of our reality can be altered in a positive way by changing our perceptions and looking at the larger context in which we live and coexist with each other and with nature.

Share your new power

When you're learning and growing, share the positive changes you're seeing. Sharing is an essential part of communicating and belonging. It helps you grow.

Connect to your higher self

Know you are not alone but in the company of a silent spiritual witness. You are accompanied by a consciousness that is higher than your conscious self. That awareness will connect you to a deeper, more essential meaning of life, which will help you to have more compassion, sensitivity, and honor. You will feel less lonely and afraid.

You won't be afraid of making sacrifices when you feel they

are necessary. Look at Gandhi and Martin Luther King, for example. They were very strong-willed people but I do not believe that they could have accomplished what they did in life if they weren't spiritual. Acknowledge your spiritual side and manifest it.

Face one fear each week

List your fears and then select one to overcome. Work on conquering that fear all week. Every single day of that week, face and confront that fear. It may be fear of fighting an injustice, improving your communication skills, or facing the fear of rejection, for example. No matter what you fear, it's better to fail and learn from your mistakes than not to try at all. So put yourself out there.

When you put all of this into action you have a twelve-step program to begin making your life the way you want it to be. The changes are no longer just in your head. You're starting to actualize them.

Reaching for Excellence

MOST OF US DO NOT ACCEPT OURSELVES. WE SPEND A LOT OF TIME and energy disguising who and what we are. We make ourselves into something that's uncomfortable and artificial. We set ourselves at odds with our beliefs and then we feel we must justify the imbalance. We feel we won't be safe until we have disguised our motives, intents, and agendas to make it seem as if we are someone else. We feel that if people know who we really are they won't accept us.

We become dishonest in our communication, and many problems result from that. Expressing fears and uncertainties is not generally admissible in our society. Showing we're afraid of something means—in our society—that we are not to be trusted. If we communicate that we aren't sure we can do a job, we won't be allowed to do it. So we have to cover up our uncertainty and appear certain, even if that's not how we feel. We've been taught to think that such a cover-up is right. But is it?

A lot of people today are sick and stressed because their actions don't reflect their feelings. This book strives to show you that many of your most closely held beliefs cause you to be imbalanced in many ways. By correcting this imbalance you can have happiness and a life that is uniquely your own—your own brand of excellence.

A lot of people wouldn't be stressed out if they realized that play is as essential as work. People have been made to feel guilty if they play, especially if they have responsibilities that are not always being met. But how many of your responsibilities are artificial? An example of artificial responsibility might include continuing to do all the cooking and cleaning up of meals when other members of the family could very easily chip in and help; or doing all the laundry, cleaning the entire house, and doing outside maintenance (gardening, cutting grass). Are these responsibilities being properly shared? In a social context, you might be the person in your Jaycees or Kiwanis Club who is always expected to do more. The person who "gets the job done." In time, people expect you to do things they very easily could help with. The whole idea of being a part of any organization or cooperative effort is to *share* responsibility. For example, would you feel guilty if you got to work on time, instead of an hour early, and left on time, instead of one half hour to one hour late.

I believe that life is for work, but not for work done only to attain things you don't need, like a color television set, a big wardrobe, a fancy car, anything fancy. I really don't want to be rich. I want a life. So while everyone else I knew was making a big income, I was making a life. I took time off to go to a Native American reservation and study their culture. I spent six years in Harlem working as a scholar and writing the first book on the psychological and social impact of African-Americans in Hollywood. I spent time writing a book called *Black Geniuses: The History of the Afro-American Experience in Inventing.* I learned about life and people. These were things I did because they were a part of living life and learning about life. They weren't mainly about making a living.

It's amazing what happens when you don't think you have to knock yourself out to make a living, when you're not going overboard on the money or success angles. You become almost like a child—in a good way. Do you ever notice that a child will play with something without the need to control it? A child doesn't have to win; she or he just likes playing. Children learn from playing.

As adults, though, most of us don't do something unless we win. We ask: What's in it for me? What am I going to get for it? How much am I going to make? Suddenly, when you make all of your time worth something, you don't want to do anything unless it has financial merit. Thus there is no time to just hang out. The people today who are dying of heart attacks are the people who have that "I need to have it in order to feel good" attitude. If you don't realize you have to make a life, not just a living, then all you will do is make a living. No matter how much of a living you make, it will never be enough to make you happy. The more you make, the more you'll spend.

Let's take a look at some ways we can rebalance ourselves. Then we can have a focus that comes from within, and reach for the kind of human excellence that transcends the limits of monetary, material, and ego-gratification considerations.

On a scale of 1 to 10, how do you rate yourself?

Look at the following areas. How do you rate yourself as these?

Adventurer

Are you bored with your life? When is the last time you did something really adventurous? It's important to be able to take risks from which you can learn, challenge yourself, and grow.

To become adventurous, you may have to break through fears, illusions, inhibitions, and expectations that can stop you. The most important thing to learn, by far, is how to give up old knowledge that is no longer relevant. I wrote a book once containing the most important information I knew at that point in my life. Four years later I wrote another book that completely contradicted the first. So I simply bought up and destroyed the remaining copies of the first. I had to let go of my old beliefs to reshape my thoughts.

When you replace old thoughts with something new and more apropos, you encourage the adventurer in you.

Parent

A parent is someone who does more than provide a place to stay and food on the table. A really good parent is also a friend, someone a child can trust and with whom a child can share his innermost thoughts, someone who won't betray the child or put him down.

A good parent encourages communication. One of the things parents can do is to ask their children, "What could we do differently to help you? Could we be more patient and understanding? Could we give you more time or be less critical? Could we develop a friendship by doing more to respect you?"

A parent also has to be able to accept criticism. Most parents are not good at this. Being in a position of power and authority, parents tend to insist on doing things their way, making their children feel powerless in the process. As a result, children learn not to speak up for themselves. They fear retaliation, overreaction, and overdiscipline. A lot of parents make the same mistakes over and over and never know it because there is never any feedback.

Parents and children need to be able to share thoughts in a safety zone. Before there is any reaction, before there is any condemning or ego-defending, children should be able to simply speak their minds freely. A parent can say, "Go ahead and tell me what you think. Tell me whether you feel what I'm doing is right or wrong. I'm not going to react to it; I'm just going to listen." Then parents can take that time just to listen and be open.

Let's say a child confronts a parent with something like this: "Mom, it's my room. You've got the whole house to keep organized and clean. I want my room to be my room. It's the only place I have that I can call my own. Let me be as messy as I want." If the mother were to react without thinking, she might say, "No, it's not your room. It's our house." That makes the child feel like a boarder in the parent's house. If the parent thought it through first, she would have time to consider her child's viewpoint and respond differently. She could then say, "I understand that you need your own space. I've been so concerned with keeping the house in order that I've been neglecting your needs." By taking a step back, you give yourself the opportunity to understand your child a lot more and to foster better communication and cooperation.

Friend

Explore your friendships. Ask your friends why they want you in their lives. Ask yourself what you like about the friendships. What do you gain from them? What would you like to be different? Are there things that annoy you about your friendships? As an example, let's say one of the things that bothers you is that every time you go out with your friends, you go where they want to go—whether to a movie, dinner, or whatever—and they rarely ask what your interests are. The assumption being their decision is good enough for both. Or you may have a friend who talks about what a great time they had the night before with some of their friends, but never invites you—and never realizes that always talking about the good time they had with other friends can make you feel left out. If it bothers you, you've got to bring it up.

Lover

I'm not talking about sexual love alone. I'm asking whether you are open to expressing and sharing the joy and inner harmony of life. Or do you see love as being exclusive? Do you say, "I love you only, and I love no one else."

We like to think that love, like everything else, is limited. But I've found that, on the contrary, there are no shortages. Although we think that everything is in short supply, really there is no limit on most things, especially love.

Why is love made exclusive? Why do you think you can only love one type of person? Why not love everyone? Think of the consequences of that. If we had been taught to love all people, could we have tolerated over two million Vietnamese civilians being killed, incinerated, and bombed out of this world or any of the seemingly endless brutal conflicts that permeate our daily lives? I think not. Life would have been seen as precious.

Teacher

We all have something to share. Think of all the lessons you have to teach others. Think of all the joy and love you can receive by giving unconditionally to others. If you honor your time instead of wasting it, you can share with people the things that you value in your life. If you had more time to get outside your home and enjoy nature, you could, for example, take your camera and indulge in some weekend nature photography. By inviting your friends, you can accomplish three things: spend more quality time with your friends, do something creative, and appreciate what it means to organize your time so that you have more time for activities you value. Another good example is attending a cultural event: most people enjoy crafts fairs, and although they don't take up much time, by freeing an extra two hours a week, you give yourself the advantage of the company and the event.

Doer

The key is not just to do things but to do things that honor real goals, real needs, and real balance. If most of what you do meets artificial goals (buy, address, and mail the perfect Halloween card to everyone you know) then you're not doing. You're filling your days to avoid doing.

I've never understood facing a problem with a problem. Negative thoughts or projections of vengeance or anger can't resolve anything. Yes, expressing anger is a natural reaction but it should be directed to allowing something to change. If I have a problem, I actively search for solutions, looking at all the possible answers I can come up with. I ask other positive people for their input as well. This is different from wanting sympathy. I want to be with someone who will help me out of my situation, someone who can make me laugh, who can put my predicament in a completely new light. Positive solutions help resolve problems.

Creator

Most people believe they aren't creative. But that's just not true. Most adults have simply forgotten how to engage in creative pursuits.

When you engage in a craft, such as weaving, painting, sculpting, or woodworking, you derive a great deal of psychological benefit. And there are thousands of classes across the country that will teach you arts and crafts. There are centers where you can learn everything from flower arranging to rebuilding car engines to remodeling homes. You can save a lot of money making things you want and doing repairs yourself. The purpose of this exercise is not merely to distract you from something that would keep you busy. We have enough busyness in our lives as it is. Rather, this provides us an opportunity to match the needs of the inner self to something in the external self that can give us greater inner peace and harmony in the way of expressing the joys of our outer life.

Most cultures pass down skills from generation to generation. Traditionally, this has been a part of our culture as well. When I was growing up, my father would fix just about anything. He would repair the car, paint the house, and lay cement block. This was a part of what parents taught children.

Many Americans see repairs as a laborious, tedious waste of time. After all, didn't we want to be successful partly so we wouldn't have to do unglamorous chores like cleaning, repairing, or maintainance ourselves? However, there's another way of looking at these jobs. In fact, one of the reasons I bought a farm—on which I toil away many of my weekends—was to actively engage in maintenance, repairs, and improvements. It is a great stress reducer; and things like planting flowers, raking leaves, or repairing a roof are all relaxing exercises. Someone from another culture—China, perhaps, or India or Japan —would find these chores to be meditative. We have mistakenly adopted the idea that only so-called productive work, work that earns us an income and enhances our career or our public position, is worthy of our time and attention. It seems, Americans have forgotten how to do for themselves. Many baby boomers, particularly in the 1980s, figured that they made enough money not to have to do things on their own. They stopped being creative and put all their energy into making more money. Specialized services proliferated for people who had the disposable income to pay for them.

Now, in the nineties, a lot of that disposable income is gone so people are having to relearn a lot of old lessons. In the process, people are noticing how economically, as well as psychologically, beneficial it is to do things for themselves.

What skills would you like to develop? What do you need to do to get started? Be creative and learn to do whatever it is you want to do.

Humanist

Quite simply, being a humanist means that you are willing to take responsibility for how your actions impact others. In effect, you're living up to higher spiritual values. Spiritual values are not necessarily associated with any religion. They simply involve being kind and ethical, i.e., not cheating, stealing, lying, committing adultery, or betraying people. These are concepts every religion recognizes, and they take you to a point where you're honoring the best that you are.

Do you take on the feelings of others?

Don't take on other people's negative feelings. Many of us are taught to believe that in order to honor our family we must take on their guilt. How many times have you gotten calls—

used as control mechanisms—intended to make you feel guilty? All you have to do is say, "Hey, I understand you're not having a good day, but I am. Good-bye." That's what I do. I won't listen to anybody else's negative comments, and I don't care who it is. My family never calls me to complain because they know I'll hang up on them. When the negative people in your life realize they can't manipulate you, they'll stop trying.

Imagine doing just the opposite, calling people to feel good and make them feel good. That would be creative and constructive.

How do you rate yourself at being?

We're always *doing* something but never thinking about ourselves simply as *beings*. What I love about visiting other cultures is seeing people who feel they don't have to do anything to be. They can just hang out. Have you ever gone to Venice, California? It's culture is based on people who are easy to be with. But we like to make fun of them, implying that these people don't have an intellect or a life. We call them flaky just because they're having fun. But they're good at being.

I've noticed this in other countries as well. The people in Trinidad, Barbados, Venezuela, and Argentina, for example, despite their differences in class and work ethic, all have something in common. They're very comfortable hanging out and being. They don't base feeling good on having something. Even people owning almost nothing have the capacity to enjoy life.

I had a wonderful time visiting some families in Jamaica. They were very poor but never allowed lack of money to get in the way of their enjoying their lives. They never used poverty as an excuse to be abusive or neglectful parents. They never dishonored their lives. I think of one woman, in particular, who had a large, wonderful family. Even though they had little materially they had a great sense of the spirit of life and never felt diminished by what they didn't have.

In our culture, we believe the lack of money causes all our problems. We think it's the reason relationships are unfulfilled. One day we'll have enough money to restore our relationships. How foolish, though, to believe that money is more important than the essence of a relationship and what you have to share. You can be just as happy poor as rich. You can start a relationship with absolutely nothing in the beginning and end up with boundless joy by just being together. Just feel the love and grace of being with another person you feel honored to be with.

When material things become all-important, you displace the importance of being together. Now you have things and debt. And the pressure of trying to meet the debt can cause you to lose the relationship.

How are you unique?

List your unique qualities. Are you able to express them or are you afraid for other people to see you as different? When you're concerned about what other people think, you edit yourself. You don't express what is naturally inside. You think, "I would allow this to come out but they're not going to like it or they might think I'm strange." Look at the average middle-class American, for example, who keeps everything within very narrow confines. Nothing is done that will in any way betray the person's middle-class ethic. What results is a very boring life.

I find the most interesting part of being with a person is his or her uniqueness. When you remember someone as being fun to be with, it is his or her unique qualities that you think of. Honor your own unique qualities. Make them important, overcoming your fear of allowing them to emerge. That will rebalance you.

Of course when you start being who you really are, some

people may reject you. You have to accept that, and remember that the most important thing is that you not reject yourself. It's your life. Outside of certain common standards set by society, there's a lot of room to be unique, fun, creative, and constructive. Why not use that room?

Do you envision what you really want?

Look carefully at what you want to change. See it in your mind. Imagine your ideal body, for example. If you were to look in the mirror, what would you like to see? (And dismiss all those images that television and magazines bombard us with. Those aren't real.) Once you know how you want to look, it's easier to find the patience and persistence to make it happen.

This holds true for all areas of your life. How do you envision your career? What do you want your home to look like? Where do you want to live? See it first to make it happen.

Three years ago a couple sat in my audience in a lecture on changing your life. She was an accountant and he was an artist. They couldn't afford living in New York nor could they see their ideals being met there. I spoke with them about what they wanted their home to look like. They shared their image and from that I suggested they consider moving to Colorado, Arizona, or New Mexico.

They wondered how to get started and I advised them to start by realizing how much they could do on their own. They didn't need to rely on any other expert because there were enough books about housebuilding to teach them what they needed to know.

They spent nine months traveling and finally found five acres of land in Arizona. It was magnificent land and not expensive because it was not near anything. Then they started reading about how to build.

They built a 7000-square-foot home with a greenhouse in it and circulating water. It was a most unique house. They spent less than $100,000 on their home; today it's worth $900,000 but they have no intention of selling it because that's where they love being. That's what they envisioned.

When you begin something, visualize what it will look like when finished. There's no shortcut to making it happen. It takes time, effort, and mastery. But it's a wonderful feeling to put time and energy into what you really want and to feel good about doing it. It's better to have a life in which you make sacrifices for your happiness than to have things and not have happiness because those things you attain have nothing to do with meeting your real needs.

When you go on vacation do you work or relax?

Most people forget what a vacation is for. A vacation is to separate your mind and body from your everyday environment. Wherever you go—mountain climbing, trail hiking, fishing, to the beach, or to an amusement park—you should be going to relax, to have fun, and to energize. If you do that you'll have a whole new sense of self-awareness when you come back.

Don't take your work problems with you on vacation, and don't take them home over the weekend. They'll interfere with the quality of your relationships with friends, family, and yourself.

Identify your filters

What mechanisms have you devised to filter out things you don't want to know about or deal with? Identify them. You've got to be aware of what's going on and you've got to deal with it.

Perhaps the first thing you need to do is to eliminate the filter of procrastination. Identify that part of you that says put it aside, hide it, disguise it, avoid it, deny it.

Yesterday, after broadcasting my show, I immediately started setting up for the next day's show so that I'd be ready to go right on the air. It gives me peace of mind knowing that I'm set up and ready to go. And why not? It only takes a few moments to set up, label tapes, and file them away.

Yet I'll go into friends' houses and find they've got their desks stacked with stuff. Books are on the floor, paper is all over the table and the other furniture. You know what I'd do in that case? I'd take everything and first sort it. Put bills and necessary papers in a pile then and throw the rest in the wastebasket. Obviously they don't need all of this stuff. Otherwise they would have dealt with it.

Here's a suggestion. Stop procrastinating. Start cleaning up one room. Take everything in the room that you no longer feel is essential to your happiness and either throw it away or give it away. Each day clean another room. Keep only what is essential. Look through your closets. You'll probably find many clothes you no longer use because you wear the same clothes over and over. Take all the things you don't wear and give them away to someone who will wear them. Give them to the Salvation Army. Better still, give them to someone on the street who needs clothes. When you stop using things with joy you lose respect for them; they just accumulate. Giving away things you don't want is a good way of feeling good about getting rid of stuff that's no longer important.

Also look at relationships you've neglected. Make a list of all the people you haven't communicated with lately whom you still would like to remain in your life, and write them a letter. Tell them why they're still important to you. I let my friends know that they are my friends, and why.

I don't believe we should ever take anyone or anything for granted. Think how many times you've done things for people who have never said thank you. Some people expect you to do certain things for them over and over. You've done it before, they assume, so you'll do it again. They forget to honor the fact that you didn't have to help them.

Stop doing things for people who have lost respect for you, because that's wasting your time and imbalancing your life.

It's better for you to give that time and energy to someone who will appreciate the gift. Plus it will make people who have taken you for granted appreciate the loss.

Do you complete projects?

Prove to yourself that you can complete things by involving yourself in a single project that will be important for your growth. Be sure to specify a goal and a reasonable timetable, and then take the steps necessary to complete it. For example, if I'm writing a book I plan in stages. There's a research phase, an interviewing phase, transcription, writing, editing. I keep track of each phase of every project on a board in my office. At any given moment I can tell you exactly where I am on any project. I never procrastinate. Every single day I work on one of my projects.

People ask me how I've written 50 books, 165 television shows, 45 documentaries, and 500 articles, and prepared 1000 workshops. I am able to do all these things because I don't allow myself to become distracted. If I start something, I finish it. I honor my word and don't make excuses for not getting the job done.

Sometimes, to complete a project, you have to master a new skill. Don't be intimidated by this. Mastering a skill may have less to do with being extremely gifted than with being relaxed in the pursuit of yourself. When you pursue yourself you're honoring your special gifts, whatever they are. You're exploring and developing your talents instead of letting uncertainties bury them.

Perhaps you would like to write a book but think, "I don't know if I can write." Well, no one starts off as a writer. I didn't come out of the womb writing. I didn't even study journalism in school. Instead, I asked a literary agent if I could work for her for free full-time. In return, she set aside three hours a week to critique my work. In the five years I worked for her I didn't earn anything, but I was able to become part of an extremely intellectually stimulating environment, which was an incomparable reward in itself. Plus each Saturday the agent would set some hours aside to go over my work. That's how I learned. I had to be willing to give up all that time at no pay in order to learn something about mastering a skill.

Are you open to change?

Most of us identify with the things we have accumulated, but these things can be easily lost. What would happen if you didn't have your possessions anymore? Has it ever occurred to you, when you see news stories of people running from bombed-out towns they've lived in all their lives, with absolutely nothing except for the clothes on their backs, that these people have got to start all over again? What would you do if you had to start over from scratch? Would you try to build the same kind of life, or would you do things differently?

If you don't think much of yourself and your ability to adapt to change, then you believe that you're not worth anything without your possessions. Your accumulations become like a ball and chain and you never get far.

When you are too attached—to things, places, or ideas— you give yourself a lot of excuses for not changing. You think you can't move because you've always lived in one place, or you can't leave a job because you've worked there for twenty years. People justify not changing by saying things like, "I've got emphysema, I got cancer, I'm stressed out, but I've got to stay at my job. In four more years, I'll get my pension. Then I can go to Florida." They have an "I've got to be taken care of" mentality.

They never think of changing by creating a job and an environment that's health-promoting. Too much conditioning and too many expectations from others get in the way.

What standards of excellence do you strive for?

Without striving for excellence and achieving mastery in at least one area of life, you will be mediocre in all things. This will lower your sense of self-esteem.

Conversely, you need to value yourself before you can concentrate your energy on purposeful goals. Attaining excellence therefore is a growth experience. If you want to take consumerist or environmental action in order to help people, for example, you can't just arbitrarily do it. You have to first prepare yourself by broadening your knowledge. Growth is not instantaneous but a gradual striving toward excellence.

Developing excellence requires change. When people want to become excellent New York City marathon runners they have to put all their energy into it. To do that they have to eliminate a lot of unhealthy habits and imbalances. If they train correctly, in six months their lives will change. They'll be able to take on challenging projects and issues, and to confront things in their lives that they never would have thought of approaching before running the marathon. The courage and strength the marathon gives them will allow them to do almost anything.

I'm suggesting you start creating excellence in one area of your life. Begin by asking, at what do I want to excel? That will provide a focus. Write on a piece of paper: Area of Excellence. Under that write down one thing at which you are going to excel, one area in which you are going to be the best you can be. Bring your focus and energy to achieving mastery in that one area of your life. Once that's achieved, focus on another area. And then on another. This way you can continue to grow.

Are your goals realistic and obtainable?

Of course you have to create realistic goals, ones that are reasonable and attainable. It's pointless to create goals that you're never going to be able to achieve.

Your goals should help you get into balance. Goals requiring excessive energy usually create imbalance; you're focusing so much energy into one area that you're neglecting other important spheres of your life. In order to create more income, for instance, you may end up imbalancing yourself nutritionally, emotionally, spiritually, intellectually, or physically.

In the process of achieving your goal, you should be able to replace negative qualities with more positive ones. If your goal is to have a healthy body, for example, take everything unhealthy out of the refrigerator and throw it away. That's step one. Then you have to take the second step—restocking the refrigerator with healthful foods. You're replacing the negative with the positive.

Set a goal for yourself of enhancing your relationships with yourself and others. Each night when you come home, instead of turning on the television or radio, set aside time for creating, for friends, for play, and for meaningful interaction with your family. You're replacing unwanted habits with more positive ones, and as a result you're creating a healthier life.

What is your legacy?

A legacy is a contribution you make to the world, something that shows you have made a difference. I believe that every human being has both the opportunity and the right to leave a legacy. Leaving a legacy doesn't mean you need to do outstanding things that the general public has to know about. You can leave a legacy in small ways. When you touch people with kindness and joy you are leaving a legacy.

Think of people who have touched your life. It's not necessarily the outstanding achievements you remember, as much as who the person is or was. Gandhi isn't remembered for being a particularly good politician. But the way he lived his life motivated a lot of people to change theirs.

Even the poorest person living in Selma, Alabama, or living in a rice field in Thailand can leave a legacy, because a legacy is not necessarily based upon materialism or wealth or education. It's often based upon what's in your heart. We have a rather distorted view of the components of success. For instance, we will look at success most often as what an individual has achieved: the accumulation of wealth, power, and control, and the public's acknowledgment of that. Generally a person becomes wealthy and can change his or her standard of living. Frequently the person has been able to achieve this success and still maintain all his or her principles. Other individuals, however, may be successful without increasing their power, control, or position and without receiving public acknowledgment. For example, they may be very healthy because they eat foods they feel will prevent disease. They may have a very fit body because they have a disciplined, focused-exercise regimen. They may have happy and healthy children, hence they have success as a parent. They may have matched their inner needs to their exterior work and therefore enjoy going to work each day. Greed and money may not be a part of their lives because they have learned not to focus on what others have, and therefore have no motivation for envy, greed, and jealousy. So in essence, they may have very successful lives. The point is that true success comes from honoring what is important to you and measuring value through your own standards, instead of an artificially created social norm.

Start thinking about what you would like to be remembered for.

Do you honor your real needs?

No two people have the same needs. Therefore, no one but you can know what your needs are. No one has the right to tell you what those needs should be. They are *your* needs.

I once had a relationship with a woman who gave me an ultimatum. Either I honor her needs or I honor my own. Our needs were different and I chose to look to my own and she became angry. That's what happens sometimes; you're not always going to please people.

I suggest you make your needs come first. Otherwise you will become imbalanced and frustrated at putting someone else's needs ahead of your own. Of course taking care of others is necessary at times, but if the other person denies your needs, and if you get into a self-denying pattern of behavior, you forget what your own needs are, and can eventually lose your sense of identity.

Begin by asking what your needs are. What do you need as a human being to feel good about yourself and to be fulfilled? Write these things down. Honor the real self rather than an artificial one; this is crucial to your well-being and happiness.

How do you keep yourself balanced?

What do you do to maintain your equilibrium in the following areas?

Intellectually

Set aside time for intellectual growth every day. Challenge your existing thoughts and knowledge. Be willing to give up ideas that can be replaced by something more relevant and vital. This will help you to grow, solve problems, and become more self-sufficient.

I suggest buying five nonfiction books, each about a different subject. Choose books that take you where you have never been before to help expand your insight. You'll start to think differently and to open yourself up to new ways of looking at life. If you read about Native Americans, for instance, you'll learn about another culture's perception of nature as sacred and you'll contrast that to European thought. This will give you a whole new perspective on environmental issues.

Each day spend one hour reading one of the books. At the end of approximately three months you will have learned something new in five different areas.

Also set aside time to learn through adult education courses. That's another way you'll be learning something new that interests you, and stretching yourself intellectually.

Environmentally

There are over twenty magazines written in lay language that inform you about environmental issues and explain how they are directly related to your health. You may have radon being emitted from your basement. You may have asbestos, formaldehyde, and bacteria in your air. Your home has the potential of being an incredibly toxic place but you won't know it unless you read up on it. Reading will help you learn how to recognize problems and know what to do about them.

Read any one of 300 books written about the environment, and subscribe to five or six magazines. That will make you aware of what is going on, how it affects you, and what you can do to help create a healthier world.

Then involve yourself in a cause that will improve the environment. Perhaps after reading you'll feel motivated, for instance, to join a local group fighting incineration. Do something to connect yourself to your world.

Physically

To improve your body, give yourself some short-term and long-term goals. Your short-term goal might be to lose a pound a week. You might want to run or walk a mile or more regularly. That will help you lose the weight, as well as increase your endurance. You might decide to go to a gym three days a week. Make a point of staying on this program.

A long-term goal might be to run or racewalk in six months. You might want to train so that a year from now you can complete a marathon.

You can also help yourself physically through detoxifying and rebalancing with good nutrition. You can rid yourself of the candida in your gut, for example, by drinking fresh raw juices, and by taking vitamin C, caprylic acid, garlic, biotin, and acidophilus cultures each day.

If you are still eating meat, you may decide you are ready to become vegetarian. You can make the change gradually by switching from meat-eating five days the first week to three days the second week. The next week you will eat meat twice and the week after that once. Then you will have no meat. Do the same for chicken and fish.

You'll start to replace the beef, chicken, and fish with more grains, beans, seeds, nuts, fruit, and juices. You'll start to take vitamins you haven't had before, such as quercetin, vitamin E, and B complex.

I balance the physical by ingesting only those foods that build health. There's never confusion about whether or not I should have sugar, meat, alcohol, caffeine, or refined carbohydrates. If foods don't honor my body, I don't eat or drink them.

In the process of seeking physical balance you can cook the most delicious recipes and interesting dishes. Your body will appreciate the creativity.

Emotionally

Are you able to express your feelings freely or do you find that you edit, change, and distort your feelings for fear that others won't accept them? If you hold back anger instead of expressing it constructively, you will only end up displacing it. It will become cancer, constipation, high blood pressure, or some other bodily ailment. If you feel some passionate feeling (and anger is part of that passion), learn to express it in a nondestructive way. People may accept or reject you for it, but you'll be doing it solely for yourself.

Choose to be with those people who support your emotional needs. If I want to be comfortable acting silly and crazy, for example, I'll be with someone who will accept this kind of behavior, not with someone who will tell me to grow up and act mature.

Spiritually

To be spiritual is to see life through a greater perspective. You realize you are part of something spiritual, whatever you want to call it—God, Goddess, universal consciousness. When you honor the spiritual self you come to realize that you are in this world to make a difference. You act in a way that respects life and you are conscious of your actions. You don't spend your time complaining, bad-mouthing, stabbing people in the back, or trying to get something for nothing.

You never intentionally hurt people and you don't act from hidden agendas; these actions would not be spiritual. Everything you do should honor the spiritual side of life.

It's easy to see how people can be negative, bitter, condescending, vile, and destructive when they are not conscious of the spirit. When you're not, everything else becomes meaningless and you have no balance. Many times I have tried helping people on a spiritual level who were not willing to help themselves spiritually or emotionally, and it was all for nothing.

How will your life be different now that you are aware of the silent witness to everything you think, say, or do? How will you do things differently?

Define the true and false parts of yourself

Your life is either working or not working based upon how in touch you are with yourself and your real needs. Recently, I spoke with a woman who was out of work. She told me that instead of running out and finding any job in her field of hospital administration, which is what she would have done only a year or six months ago, she was taking the opportunity of having time to match her real self with a job that meets her real inner needs.

The job she chooses may not be in hospital administration. She realized that her experience in that field taught her that she is more interested in working with people than with statistics and budgets. As a result she will expand her options. Making important changes requires knowing the truth about who you are. If this woman didn't have a sense of who she is, she would just take the first job to come along.

In looking at who you are, don't get too caught up in trying to figure out where you went wrong. There won't ever be enough therapists to help you resolve what went wrong in your background. The current fad, for instance, is to blame dysfunction on sexual abuse. Just about everyone in America has now been sexually abused, it seems. That's why their lives don't work. They're sure of it. They've heard it on Oprah.

The truth becomes grossly exaggerated. Of course there are abuses, but everyone shouldn't be using that as an excuse to put off having a life. You're either completely dysfunctional, in which case you should be in Bellevue, or you're functional, in which case you should give up living in the past and have a life now. If we're afraid of actualizing, we use our background as an excuse. Our parents become the reasons for our limiting our lives. That's a cop-out.

Get in touch with your real identity by looking at what works and what doesn't work in your life. Are you in a job that you really don't like? Are you in relationships that don't meet your needs? Let go of the beliefs that keep you from being yourself. Start looking for ways you can actualize your real identity. And remember not to overlook any part of your life that works; rather, appreciate it, honor it, and focus on it. Don't replace that.

What fits and what doesn't?

When you're in the right place, in the right job, and with the right people, you feel as though everything fits. You feel comfortable and natural. There's a rhythm to life and you feel that you're in the flow of things.

You know when things don't feel right. When relationships don't work, for example, it's not because one person is to blame. No one has to be wrong. It may just be that two people don't fit together. You can have a good job but it may not be the right job for you. You don't have to blame the job.

An attorney friend of mine was always feeling hyper, critical, negative, bitter, and cynical until he changed his circumstances. Now he's practicing law but a completely different type of law. He left New York and now lives in Seattle in an environment that fits his needs. He's become a completely different human being.

Think back about the people and places you've most enjoyed. What made you feel so naturally good? Where do you feel you belong? Where you feel the best is where you should be. Start preparing yourself to be there instead of sitting around and yearning for that place. It takes time, but you can begin to prepare yourself now for where you really want to be and what you really want to do.

Describe and define conflicting realities in your life

Figure out where your life is out of balance. Only then can you rebalance it. Be honest. It's easy to deceive yourself. You get so used to your life being a certain way that you begin to believe you don't know how to change. You start to believe you can't when you can.

Ask yourself who in your life is trying to define your reality by keeping you exactly the way you are. People tend to want to keep you from changing when they want to maintain the power structure of a relationship. In the process, they try to keep you away from your path. You've got to recognize this and stop it. Then you'll be able to choose a more fulfilling and rebalanced life.

Finding Happiness

PEOPLE CONSTANTLY SEEK HAPPINESS FROM SOME EXTERNAL PANACEA but they never quite grasp it. They have moments of joy, but are not able to sustain it. In the absence of happiness, everything becomes an issue. Your energy, instead of being spent on the enjoyment of life, is spent on meaningless chores.

How much time and energy do you spend on things that aren't significant? Do you make insignificant tasks significant because you're looking for something that's missing? What's really lacking is the honoring of the inner self. The questions in this chapter are designed to help you understand what prevents you from finding happiness. If you sort through all the obvious problems and deal with them one at a time, you'll slowly come to grips with the reasons for your unhappiness.

How do you justify or resolve pain from your past?

Look for ways in which your past conditioning might limit your happiness. For example, you might crave physical affection, just a pat on the back or a hug from a friend, but you don't allow yourself to give or receive it because you were taught not to seek or initiate physical displays of emotion. Perhaps you're a man, and you were led to believe that it was necessary to project a masculine, stoic image all the time. Now you're denying yourself an experience you need because you were taught it was wrong. This can be especially isolating.

You can limit yourself in more subtle ways as well. Perhaps

you would like to share your feelings with someone, but you prevent yourself from doing so because you fear rejection. You may avoid closeness because you trusted someone in the past and were hurt. Perhaps you confided in a friend who later used what you said against you. That experience may have taught you to guard yourself.

Maybe you learned to deny yourself happiness by living your father's or mother's dreams, instead of your own. Perhaps you're a man who wanted to be a musician but your parents wanted you to become a doctor. They scolded you and made you feel unmasculine for your interest in music. As a result you learned to put on a facade by acting very masculine and overachieving in business, sports, or some other area. You repressed the genuine, sensitive side of your nature because you feared it would be used against you. And you may still be holding on to pain from the past.

Stifling your true self might keep you from getting hurt again, but it also prevents you from experiencing real joy. You lose sight of inner qualities that make you special. You seek approval from the world by acting cool, dressing a certain way, or buying fancy cars. You're looking for happiness outside of yourself, but that kind of happiness can only be momentary.

Being unhappy is emotionally toxic. You've got to eliminate the toxins before you can rebuild your health. Only then can you change. You don't rebuild your health by bringing in something new without eliminating the old.

Many people in our society don't understand this. The style is to be super-hip and try something new—a new twelve-step program, a new self-help group. Everybody wants to take a shortcut to the new without first resolving the old. But nothing changes that way. You just plaster another layer on top of an already overburdened psyche and push the real you further down.

First examine your current patterns of behavior. Ask yourself where they come from. How are they getting in the way of your happiness? What real needs are you denying yourself?

How can you let go of old patterns that keep your life from working? What first step can you take to validate who you really are?

What have you relinquished to gain a better standard of living?

Most people buy the American dream. They believe that happiness is external and they want materialistic success. Thus they organize their daily lives around making money and tend to spend more than they have on things they don't really need. But concentrating on what money can buy often creates an insatiable desire for bigger and more expensive things.

Whole relationships can be centered around the attainment of tangible things, such as cars, houses, more money. Many couples make these things the focus of their being together; they believe they are being responsible and showing loyalty by giving things to their partner. One wonders what would happen to the relationship without the things? Would the people involved no longer have a basis for being together?

I've lost many friends over the years who felt they needed to upgrade their lifestyles once they started making a little money. They directed all of their creative energies toward this purpose and, in the process, gave up valuable time and energy. They stopped having time for themselves or their friends, time to take trips, time to read, study, and engage in hobbies. They gave it all up to work long hours for a "better" standard of living.

People are terrified of the idea of lowering their standard of living. Couples feel miserable because they can't buy a house. This is really peculiar to my way of thinking because not owning a home means greater freedom from debt. When you receive your paycheck at the end of the week it's yours to save or to spend on more important things. And the purchase of a vacation home is another questionable thing, from my point of view. Rather than buy a house in the country that you feel obligated to go to every week, you could travel first-class and visit places you've always wanted to see.

I frequently counsel people who can't figure out why they're unhappy after attaining all the trappings of material success. The problem is they've lost touch with the essence of who they are, as well as with the ability to really relate to others. Most of their conversations, for example, are about how well or how poorly they are doing, in a material sense. And they never ask how *you* are.

As a child growing up in a small town in the South, I remember watching the old men sitting around and whittling away. They wouldn't carve anything in particular and they wouldn't say fifteen words in a day. There was a sense of contentment, though, a feeling of camaraderie. They had an idea of what life was about, why they were alive, and what they wanted to do with their lives. They were doing it. They knew how to just *be*. The key is to appreciate being alive.

Today this scene is hard to find in our society. Most people rush frenetically from task to task. They communicate superficially and then wonder why nobody understands their essential needs.

Think of all the things that you consider essential. Are they really? Do you look at what you don't have and think that acquiring those things will make you happy? Does thinking about the things you don't have cause you stress? Have you acquired a "successful" lifestyle and given up a happier way of life?

What generates happiness?

What is happiness? Health? Love? Good friends? A nice place to live? Creative expression? Freedom? Inner peace? All these things are important. Who creates them, and where do they come from? You do, and they come from inside.

You are happiest when you are living up to your own expectations. Living according to other people's expectations limits you. If peer pressure dictates that I must have a family to be happy, then without a family I should be unhappy. Accordingly, if I don't have a love in my life, then I will be unhappy.

Why is it, then, that as a single male I'm so happy? The reason is I live according to my own ideals. I know what is essential to my own happiness, and it doesn't depend on other people's expectations. Happiness starts with health of mind, body, and spirit, and a sense of inner peace.

You need to restructure your life so that you have time for what is important to you. Start with the idea of freedom from obligations, of being responsible first to yourself. That gives you the freedom to be. Each day gives you only twenty-four hours. But if you use your energy to change your life, you can make those hours work for you.

In my daily life, I use my time to my advantage and only share energy with people who honor me. I'm working on a book project, for example. I met with a publisher last week but rejected his offer because I realized I would be doing a lot of work for nothing.

Later I found another, smaller publisher and decided to work with him. This person wanted to work with me and planned to help with the editing and research. When another person cooperates on a project there's a constructive effort that makes the project happen twice as fast and with half as much difficulty. He's on my side and we're working together. I chose that.

My agent reminded me that I wasn't going to make any money with this publisher, but that didn't deter me in the least. My life is not just about money. It never has been and it never will be. It's about what is going to make me happy.

Ask yourself, are you generating your own happiness or living according to the expectations of others?

How can you make each day exciting?

Start the day by listing all the things you would like to do that day. It doesn't matter if you get to them all.

Here's what I do. No matter what, I set aside two hours a day to work out. My body counts. If I don't take care of it, it will become dysfunctional. I don't want to end up with cancer or heart disease.

I make time for my friends each day as well. They're important to me; I don't like to have a friend in name only. Therefore, I allow myself a minimum of two hours a day for my friends.

I also set aside time to pursue cultural interests. I live in a city with wonderful museums, theaters, and concerts. How in the world can I live in New York and not take advantage of these things?

Scholarship is important to me. Every day I spend six hours studying. When I study I engage my mind. The more I learn, the better able I am to teach. Find me a teacher who continues being a student, and I'll show you a good teacher.

Every day I take a walk in the park. There I am totally relaxed and not thinking about anything in particular. I'm living in the moment by just being.

Of course there must be time for work, food, doing the laundry, and all the other responsibilities I have. It all gets done without hurrying and scurrying. I make time each day for fun, for seriousness, for friends, and for the body and the mind. One of the reasons that people do not have a lot of energy—and as a result, much positive activity—when they get home from work is that they're tired. And, realistically, what are you going to do if you're tired? Eat, sit in front of the TV, then go to bed.

To gain more energy, I would suggest starting with the basics, like a thyroid test. You can test your thyroid in the morning, before you even get out of bed. Put an oral thermometer under your armpit for ten minutes, each morning for three consecutive days. If your temperature is below 97.5, then you may well have an underactive thyroid. Other symptoms include intermittent depression with no apparent cause; thinning of hair and dryness of skin; and cold hands and feet.

A second possible cause of fatigue is exhaustion of adrenals, overuse of sugar and caffeine, and stress. In this case you should have a complete physical; or go to a chiropractor, who might do kinesiology testing to determine the health of your adrenals. Taking B-complex vitamins (50 milligrams twice daily for two weeks) and vitamin C (1000 milligrams five times daily) will certainly help improve overall adrenal function.

Overeating at lunch, especially if you also consume alcohol or foods that you may be sensitive to, can cause brain fatigue. One way to discover whether food sensitivities are a factor in your tiredness is to undergo a one-week rotation diet: eliminating all the foods you commonly eat and replacing them with different ones. For example, if yours is a wheat-heavy diet, replace all wheat products with rice. Switch from sodas to juice. And try to eat smaller, more frequent meals, because hypoglycemia is the most common cause of afternoon fatigue. But fatigue may also be caused by intestinal parasites (giardia, for example) and by the presence of electromagnetic radiation —such as that emitted by computer screens.

On a nonphysical level, we always know when we're excited by something: When we have something to look forward to, we have more energy, and invest our days with some project, craft, or activity that we know will keep us stimulated and enthusiastic.

What I don't do is as important as what I do. I don't waste my time. I don't spend time whining, complaining, kvetching, looking for the ideal relationship, and talking fifteen times a day on the phone about things that don't matter. I don't waste time watching television unless there is something specific that I want to see. Thus I have time to structure my life around what I want and need to do to feel healthy and fulfilled.

You may think that you don't have the time to integrate all the things you want to do into one day. Once you realize how many unnecessary responsibilities you've been taking on, you will find time to do the things that are important to you. You must not spend time doing things just because other people expect you to. For example, are you always cleaning another person's room? Do you cook for others and do their laundry? If they're over five years old, why not let them start taking care of themselves? Even youngsters can do simple tasks— making beds or sorting laundry for instance. Doing things for other people unnecessarily takes time away from yourself. You're letting other people waste your time.

Families can waste your time the most: specifically you need to address adult family members who like to spend time complaining. If, instead of asserting your need to be somewhere else, you assume they have the right to make demands of you, a lot of your time is going to be eaten up by negativity. Let complainers know that you don't want them wasting your time. That doesn't mean you don't love them. It means that the time you spend with them should be quality time. You don't want to argue, complain, blame, or gossip.

Until you realize how much time is wasted in a day, you cannot appreciate how much time you have. Simply eliminate all wasted time. Don't engage in gossip. Don't let people talk to you for more than a few minutes on the phone. Don't let people share negativity with you.

When you spend time with the important people in your life, really *be* with them. Use that time constructively, not just to vent problems.

Write a positive affirmation each day about why the day counts. Every day should be exciting; there is something wrong with living only for the weekend. So make the priority you. Build the day around your needs. Make yourself count. Justify your journey.

Are you secure in your identity?

People often keep themselves from rewarding careers and limit their creative expression because of what someone else has said. Perhaps one person once told you that you aren't smart enough, and you still believe it. Or maybe someone says you're an old woman and you take it to heart. You start to act and dress like you're old, not because this is the real you, but because of someone else's expectations.

Realizing you are free to grow and be who you are can reverse the self-limitation process. People from every walk of life succeed far beyond the expectations of others. You find them in every profession. And if they can do it, why can't you?

First, you need to feel secure in your identity. You need to affirm who you are and to get in touch with what you believe in. Then others won't be able to deter you from your convictions.

Have the courage to express yourself every day even if that means people are going to abandon you for it. It's better to be alone than with others who don't understand or accept you as you are.

People who live their lives as I do have been denigrated for years and years as health nuts, quack promoters, charlatans, scam artists, people who only want to manipulate the public with false ideas about eating right. There are those who have wanted us denied, dismissed, or destroyed. What if we took them seriously? We would never be able to stand up for our principles and live healthy, productive lives.

Do you allow yourself to be the target of other people's insensitive statements? Do you internalize what people say and keep yourself from following your dreams and goals, and from reaching your potential? If so, it's time to affirm where you want to go in life and who you want to be. If you allow others to see who you really are you will attract like-minded, positive people. Believe in yourself, persevere, and you will succeed.

How much of your real self do you share?

Relationships are a lot more exciting when you let the real you out. Work on that. Let who's really in there out. Forget about your image. Forget about what you've manicured. Forget about what you've let people believe is the real you. Let people see what you're really about. Let the real you come out. As an example: Let's say you have an interest in sports, but because your friends have a certain image of you, you haven't made time to participate—even though you really want to be active, not a spectator. Well, tell your friends that you're getting involved in some sport, be it basketball, volleyball, softball, skiing, skating, or whatever, and ask them to participate with you—then schedule it. Another example might be that you've always been perceived as a jock, but you have a romantic, sensitive side that you've hidden from others: reading poetry, perhaps, or writing.

Do you appreciate beauty in yourself, in others, and in life each day?

Seek out the beauty in life. Notice what is good and beautiful in yourself, in others, and in life. You let beauty into your life by acknowledging the beauty that exists all around you. Otherwise, you only see ugliness, which justifies your feeling cynical. It's your choice. Why not allow the beauty in?

What do you do in excess?

Excesses of anything are signs of imbalance. Identify extremes and start to decrease or eliminate them. The following behaviors, when excessive, can lead to disharmony of body, mind, and spirit.

Worrying

Nothing constructive comes from worrying; you just get sick doing it. When you worry you waste time agonizing over things that probably won't happen, although when you actively imagine a worst-case scenario over and over again, you may actually contribute to its occurrence.

Look for solutions to your situations instead of worrying about them. You can avoid ten hours of worry by spending ten minutes looking for a possible answer. Simply think: This situation doesn't feel good. I'm going to find a way to change it.

Working

Our society values excessive work and discounts the idea of living to enjoy life. A friend of mine used to be a successful investment banker but one day gave that up to become a gardener. He gave up an enormous salary, which greatly upset his family.

I once took a trip with this friend. Everybody I met through my friend on that trip treated him like a bum, even though he is a gentle, kind, and loving man. He doesn't overwork but when he does work he's a wonderful and patient gardener. He may sit for hours before deciding where he wants to plant something, but everything he plants grows. He's designed and built beautiful meditation gardens.

Let us remember what life and happiness are about.

Fantasizing

Fantasizing unrealistically wastes valuable time and energy. It is easy to fall into the trap of believing you will never find a better way of life, and using fantasies to escape the drudgery of life instead of eliminating your dissatisfaction with your days.

On the other hand, it's good to fantasize about something

reasonable and obtainable. Daydreaming allows you to extend yourself and to reach for more than you currently have. Realistic fantasies help you to grow, to have a more interesting life, and to feel good about yourself.

Replaying past experiences

Replaying past experiences over and over again is counterproductive. You have a life today; you don't need to live in the past. To make your life important, don't dwell on yesterday's memories. This keeps you stuck in a time warp and prevents you from living more fully now.

One thing you can do to make your life happen now is to create a project for yourself. Engage in something you've never done before and take responsibility for its completion. This means that you are going to have to stretch yourself intellectually, creatively, and emotionally, with discipline and focus. Whatever the project, give some time and attention to it each day. When it's complete, accept whatever it is as successful. The habit of creating something new every day allows you to rejuvenate and to acknowledge your powers in the present. Thus every day has meaning.

People ask me why I create documentaries, write books, and engage in multiple other projects. I love the passion of living in the moment. Once I finish a project, however, it's part of yesterday, and I'm on to the next project.

Notice your thoughts. Do they tend to drift into the past or stay in the present? What projects are you involved in currently? What can you start doing that you've only thought about up til now?

Making wrong choices

Do you make wrong choices over and over? You start to know in advance that you're going to regret your decision but you make it anyway because of fear or denial. Perhaps you want to go out dancing but repeatedly turn down a friend's offer. Later that night you eat a quart of ice cream out of frustration and anger with yourself.

Nothing happens unless you make it happen. To start making right choices for yourself, begin by letting go of old behaviors that no longer work for you. Take a chance on life. How many times, for example, have you heard someone say, "Things will get better." Things only get better when you pursue a course of action to allow things to get better. In one case, a man I know had a dysfunctional relationship with his daughter. They bickered constantly, and the daughter grew up to react strongly against her father, who was hypercritical: Nothing she did ever seemed to be good enough. The daughter did all the rebellious things she could—keeping their home messy, inviting men she knew her father would find unacceptable, even going so far as to sell some drugs while in college. Clearly she was reacting in a negative, self-destructive way. I suggested that one of the problems was that for as long as I knew him, his daughter had to compete for affection with the other women in his life—and the women always seemed to come first. Therefore when a meeting was held to help them reconcile the wrong choices they both had made, I suggested they spend their weekends together. Both agreed it was a good idea. The very next weekend he told me he was going to spend the afternoon with his daughter but his evening with his girlfriend. I said, "Start making the right choices. Spend the day and the evening with your daughter, take her to dinner and a play, not your girlfriend. The girlfriend will be there after your daughter is gone." His first reaction was to deny it would make a difference to his daughter. I said, "What do you expect? You have been excluding her for so long, she will probably say nothing, but she will feel rejected and not see you as a new person willing to grow. Why not be with her alone so she doesn't feel competition?" Finally the message broke through. He was able to let go of an old behavior that is no longer working for him.

Let go of old expectations. They only limit you. In my running club on Sunday mornings, I tell people to focus their minds on what they want to do and to allow their bodies to go to where they feel good and comfortable. Sooner or later they always go further and faster than they ever thought they would.

Depending on relationships

Can you enjoy life without someone else, or do you depend on relationships to make you feel happy? Do you live through someone else? Are you overly concerned with how others feel about you? In other words, are you holding others responsible for how you feel about yourself? Or are you able to honor your individual needs and still find positive things to share with another person? Achieving that kind of balance exemplifies a healthy relationship.

Taking on too much responsibility

Being excessively responsible shows that you don't feel acceptable for who you are; you have to prove you are acceptable by the things you do. If you're excessively responsible, you might be the type of person who does everything for everybody—walks their dogs, does their laundry, takes care of their children, and so on. People start to take advantage of you; they think they can always count on you for everything. In the process, you may forget to be responsible for yourself and you will forget how to enjoy life.

Of course there are appropriate responsibilities. You need to be responsible to society and unselfish in the pursuit of life. You must do things that will help others in some way. Giving time and service to those in need is an important part of honoring the spiritual side of our nature.

Searching

I strongly believe we should spend time searching—but not excessive time. Many people are always searching and the irony is they don't even know what they're searching for—

they're just engaged in a constant search. I don't believe Ivan Boesky or Michael Milkin knew what they were really looking for. They each had a billion dollars—enough for lifetimes of spending—but couldn't stop their yearning for more even if what they were doing was illegal.

There's a time when we have to ask ourselves, where is our journey taking us? What are we looking for? Perhaps we need to look inside instead, to come to grips with who we are.

Regretting

Many people ponder, "If only ... if only ... if only." For example, how many people regret not becoming an athlete? Instead they're weekend warriors who hang out at bars and root for teams. Not that it's wrong to root for a team and to have fun with sports. It's fun to have your heroes and favorites. That's normal. But not when it's excessive.

People who feel they've never won anything, because they've never tried anything, tend to live through movie heroes—Arnold Schwarzenegger, Sylvester Stallone, Clint Eastwood. These heroes are always loners facing insurmountable odds and winning; while sitting in the theater audience members feel like a hero vicariously but when the lights go up it's easy to feel a deflated sense of self.

There's a better way of dealing with regret at having lost opportunities than watching movie heroes. It's called taking action now.

Have You Experienced Unconditional Love?

Being able to love someone unconditionally is a direct result of whether or not you received that kind of love from your parents and other significant people in your life.

Children need the freedom to fail. This teaches them to take chances in life, and, more importantly, that they are acceptable for who they are, and not judged according to what they can do. I came home from school once with a B on my report card. My mother looked at it and asked me, "What didn't you like about your teacher?" I said I was just bored with the class and she let it go at that. I wasn't made to feel bad about it.

Parents can manipulate children into believing the children owe them A's with such comments as, "If you don't get A's you're not going to get into the right school and you won't get ahead in this world. We're working ourselves to death so that you can go to Princeton or Harvard but we can't do this without your help. You're not respecting what your mother and I are doing to get you through this."

Suddenly the child feels terrible. He or she has been made to feel as if he's betrayed his parents, and that he's a selfish, no-good person. Putting these unnecessary responsibilities on a child tells him or her that succeeding—not happiness—is the priority.

Parents need to ask themselves, are we just as positive and encouraging when our children get F's as opposed to A's? Good parents are.

What Does Your Life Revolve Around?

Answering this question will help you determine whether your life is focused or aimless. Ask yourself, does your life revolve around work? Relationships? Obsessing? Food? Play? Future happiness? Game playing? Changing another person or some circumstance? If your life revolves around trying to control the world around you, you won't ever know what it is to be happy.

The fact is, you can't make others change the outer reality. I learned some time ago that I can't change the AMA, the food industry, and the minds of the people who are undermining our health. Of course that doesn't mean I can't do something on my own to try to affect the world.

What I can do is take action. If the rich won't help the poor I can find ways to do it. I needn't be rich to help them, just kind and giving. I can't make other people stop polluting the environment, but I can stop polluting it, and set an example for others. Although I can't keep bankers and corporations from persuading people to buy things they don't need, I can respect that money properly used can help people. I can choose to make money only one vehicle for change in my life and not the center of it. I can buy only what I really need. I can't make other people stop complaining, but I can make sure I don't become like them. I can wake each morning honoring life, valuing my day on the planet, and using my time to develop character.

So you see, while I can't always alter what's out there, I certainly can control what's in my heart. I can generate unconditional self-love and other inner qualities that make life worth living: the innocence, honesty, and playfulness of the child that remains in me, as well as unconditional love, kindness, acceptance, patience, and reverence. Then there is no need for unhappiness.

Finding Security

OUR SOCIETY REVERES HIGH-LEVEL ACHIEVERS. BUT RARELY DO WE ask, what is the purpose of achieving all that? What are you trying to prove? What's missing in your life for you to devote so much of your time to this success chase? Why do you always need more?

During the 1980s a large portion of the baby boom generation was engaged in doing as much with their education and careers and lifestyles as they could. But they never stopped to think whether life had a purpose outside of attaining things. They never realized that they were covering up an insecurity.

The symptoms were there—the workaholism, the cocaine use, the spending that got people into debt—but no one saw the signs. Society welcomed these high-level achievers, and the baby boomers themselves didn't think anything was wrong with their approach to life. People who are succeeding at whatever they are doing generally don't see themselves as dysfunctional. To the contrary, they congratulate themselves on taking every opportunity that comes their way.

What legacy have these people left? Today, every major corporation in America—including IBM, AT&T, chemical companies, and pharmaceutical companies—is eliminating thousands and thousands of jobs. People are now beginning to save money and not buy things they don't need. People are learning some hard lessons. They're trimming down.

The people who lost their homes, went into bankruptcy, and became loaded down with excessive debt are very insecure people. A lot of them have gone into recovery programs such as self-help and 12-step programs and therapy, to understand why they didn't take time for themselves, their families,

80

and their physical, emotional, and spiritual health. They're analyzing why they spent all their time making money.

They were substituting money for self-esteem. It made them feel secure. It made them feel that they *were* somebody. But it doesn't work that way—not in the long run.

Guess who really had self-esteem. Guess who wasn't insecure. Guess who wasn't spending money they didn't have on things they didn't need just to prove they were okay. The people who we thought were the losers, the people we thought weren't hip and stylish, weren't shakers and breakers of the world—our Depression-era families, our aging moms and dads. When the boom hit they didn't sell their homes to get new homes. They were happy with the homes they had. Yet many were insecure because of the eleven years of the Great Depression. But they became more stable, appreciated everything they had because of what they endured.

As a result, these people own their own mortgage-free homes today. They're able to live off modest incomes and have money in the bank. They can enjoy their lives and spend quality time with one another.

A lot of the baby boomers with their MBA's, after all is said and done, have less financial stability than their parents. It goes to show that money is just a substitute for the security people feel they need. When security is lacking, money is spent to fill the void. When security is there, money is not used to prove anything. It's seen in a different, more utilitarian, perspective.

How did you entertain yourself before you had money?

A friend of mine confided in me that he wasn't happy because he was broke. "What used to make you happy before you had money?" I asked. We spoke awhile and I realized that it wasn't the lack of money that was making him unhappy; it was his mindset. I reminded him that if you don't have money to entertain yourself, you've still got you.

Think about the enjoyable times you've had without money. What did you do? Perhaps you engaged in hobbies or spent time reading. Sixty percent of all Americans never read a book after high school. Thirty percent read only one book a year. They stop reading because they don't have to; they forget how enjoyable reading is.

Without money you may have spent more time with friends or family. Maybe you traveled and played. Most people need more time for play.

List ways to enjoy life without money.

How does a lack of security affect you?

Notice how a lack of security affects the following areas of your life:

Relationships

When you lack security within yourself, your relationships suffer. You feel victimized, depressed, and fearful. Somehow, you think you're not worthy, and that comes across to others.

You may place more emphasis on material success and your image than on people. Being yourself and relating honestly is not good enough. You brag about your children: "My son is a doctor." You ask friends, "How much did your engagement ring cost?" or "How much did that car set you back?" You judge people by how much they have and what they can do for you. You talk about money all the time. You think, "I shouldn't be happy and playing. I should be earning more money to have more security."

Where you live

A lot of people refrain from moving to a new locale because they want to maintain a certain lifestyle and stay connected to the people they know. Giving that up provokes anxiety. It means readjusting their self-image.

It becomes especially difficult to lower one's standard of living. Today, because of the economic situation, we have more people going from middle class to lower middle class than ever before, but downscaling is not easy to do if you identify yourself with how you live.

Scheduling

When you feel secure you schedule your time differently than you do when you feel insecure.

When you feel secure, you plan time for personal growth. You make time for play, relating, introspection, meditation or prayer, joy, and friendship. You organize your day around what is essential to your happiness.

When you feel insecure you will generally devote each day to earning money. The trouble appears when you start giving up all your time in pursuit of the dollar and you neglect your family and friends. You don't get to see your children grow. Before you know it, they're gone. Life loses its meaning. One day you wake up and look in the mirror and you're old. You wonder where the years have gone. You regret not having used your time more wisely.

Time is a precious commodity; in fact it's priceless. So do something with your time that acknowledges its value. If you enjoy art, spend an afternoon visiting a museum. If you enjoy music, go to a concert. Make time for friends. Take your children to a puppet show. Have the confidence to live your day in a way that will enhance your life.

Freedom to experience all aspects of living

When you feel insecure you cannot fully experience life. You lack confidence and are afraid to take risks.

Society encourages this risk-fearing attitude. You're supposed to maintain the status quo, to work for monetary success and never see possibilities beyond that. You are expected to become addicted to the things that money can buy and go into debt over them.

If you're like most people, you buy into this prescribed way of life because it's supposed to make you happy. Instead, though, it makes you less and less free, and the very things you thought would make you happy keep you imbalanced.

To be free, you need to go outside the boundaries of predictability and try something completely new. No one can tell you how far you're supposed to go or what you're supposed to feel. There's no feedback; you just have to experience and become the architect of your life.

Examine how completely you experience and enjoy the following areas of your life.

SEX

When you feel secure about yourself, you are free to experience your sexuality. You are willing to try things that you wouldn't otherwise try.

You are never told to have happy sex. No two people think of sex in the same way—differing perceptions are based on the messages received from parents, religious authorities, friends, teachers, and the various media. Confusion occurs when what should be a pleasurable experience between two consenting adults is tainted with fear on one side and guilt on the other: Fear because what you're experiencing is condemned by parents, religion, and society, which causes shame and brings up childhood guilt because "good little boys and girls don't do that." Which in turn creates an artificial constraint—a sort of psychic chastity. How much more would you do or allow yourself to feel if you were not constrained by fear? In my experience, most people live with far less sexual pleasure than they are capable of, and sublimate their passion by reading books like *The Bridges of Madison County,* watching pornographic or explicit films, or obsessing about the exploits of Madonna and other more liberated celebrities. Whereas someone with a healthy, fulfilled sex life will be much more interested in his or her own exploits than those of other people, most repressed individuals will pay obscene amounts of money, give unlimited publicity to and keep focused attention on public, frequently exhibitionistic displays, in order to relive their sexual fantasies and pleasures.

So, after experiencing pleasure followed by guilt, what now? Should you deny the pleasure? Who could you tell? Those who will listen are more likely to listen to your stories with a feeling of envy or jealousy, and then adopt the moral high ground, perhaps admonishing you—but probably bad-mouthing you and backstabbing you. There is nothing worse than this sort of betrayal of trust. It might be better, I think sometimes, to put everything on video—call it the "No More Confidences Channel." Because everyone seems ready to betray everyone else, especially when *Hard Copy* is ready to buy the story. It makes you realize that you'd better not share anything you don't want others to know about—otherwise, chances are that everyone will know, sooner or later.

Could you imagine suddenly having the freedom to experience sex the way you want to instead of playing by the rules? You could explore and let go of all the preconditioned notions of how sex should affect you. You could stop thinking about what's right or wrong. You would no longer be limited by what your class says you can do. Instead, you would express the feelings you have without fear of condemnation.

CREATIVITY

When you feel secure you are free to express and experience creativity. There are no limits to what you can do. Don't acknowledge limits just because you are told to. They'll keep you locked in a nonproductive mode. Decide what feels right to you. For example, I sleep two hours a night. If I were to follow the norm I'd be sleeping eight hours even though I don't need to. I'd have less time to create. I also take certain nutrients during training for a faster recovery. If I were to listen to the advice of physicians who say that nutrition doesn't matter, I would be limiting myself as an athlete.

If you accept limits imposed on you, you lose your creativity and spontaneity. You never go beyond artificial boundaries. Ask yourself what limits keep you from being who you want to be and remove those constraints from your life. Give yourself what you need in order to be more creative.

INTELLECT

Intellectual freedom allows your mind to process and understand new concepts. You discard fixed notions of how things should be and start looking at things from an enlightened, expanded perspective. You are open to seeing things the way they are, and not limited to a biased viewpoint.

I watched a television show featuring Dr. Anthony Fauci who said megavitamins have nothing to do with health. They don't help the immune system, he said, therefore they cannot help people with AIDS. I'm sure he believes that, even though it is a false statement. The problem is that, intellectually, he's not free. His beliefs are fixed. He thinks that only chemotherapy or a vaccine can stop the AIDS virus because he hasn't been open to looking at the evidence to the contrary that's been piling up.

I would offer a different perspective from that of Dr. Fauci, one based on the evidence provided by the experience of many individuals. From this I can see that antioxidants have made a great deal of difference in AIDS treatment, both in terms of delaying the onset of AIDS from HIV, and lessening the devastating effects of the illness. But in order to appreciate the value of antioxidants, you have to approach the subject using a different type of therapeutic model than the one Dr. Fauci is familiar with. And it's not unusual for a person to be down on what he's not up on.

People have a mistaken notion that as long as you have a degree—an M.D. or a Ph.D.—you automatically have intellectual insight. That is absolutely wrong. I've met people who have never been to college who possess a greater intellect than people holding advanced degrees. They're not confined to one belief; they're breaking through old paradigms and establishing new ones. And that's how we progress intellectually. That's how Einstein dissolved the notion of Newtonian physics and developed quantum physics. That's how Enrico Fermi was able to split the atom. Their intellects weren't limited by the traditional thinking of their time.

Middle-class people are not encouraged to be intellectual although society says upper-middle-class and upper-class people can be. In truth, of course, intellect has no class. Never believe that you are as smart as people have told you. Believe you are smarter.

TRAVEL

We can travel anywhere. We can see our own city. We can see our own country. We can see the world. But I know people living in New York City who have never seen what New York has to offer. They limit what they'll experience.

When you free your mind then you free yourself to experience any place, and you get a completely new perspective on life.

LEARNING ABOUT OTHER BELIEFS

When you are free to experience other beliefs you get to learn from people with a completely different outlook on life. That will either enhance or challenge your own beliefs.

In order to be open to experience other beliefs, you have to be willing to let go of your own fixed ideas. Being closed-minded is a very dangerous thing. It causes you to become anti-cultural and nationalistic. It makes you unable to benefit from other cultures. If you visit other countries but see only the tourist attractions, you're missing the most important aspect of travel—getting to know people who lead lives different from yours.

Do you equate security with being overly responsible?

Most people believe that if they have failed to meet their responsibilities they have failed at life. Other people look down on them and criticize them. I expected so and so, they say, and you let me down. You didn't provide. You're supposed to be this, you're supposed to be that.

Now the person feels a tremendous sense of guilt. Now he or she is motivated for the wrong reasons: guilt and fear. That drives him into desperation and frequently traumatizes him. It ties him up so he can't do anything, or it drives him to succeed in ways that are excessive. The person may become compulsive and addicted to appearing responsible.

How many people do you know who are overly responsible? They never know how to say no. They always take on the responsibilities of everyone else, and rarely take time out for themselves.

Are you using your skills to your best advantage?

A good way to find greater security and happiness is to use and develop new skills. Sometimes this means using them in creative ways. To give you an example, a graphic artist, working in a major clothing store in New York City, told me that he wanted to make a career change but that he didn't know what he wanted to do. He said that outside of graphic arts he didn't believe there was anything else he could do.

I helped him review his situation. He discovered that it

wasn't his skill that was making him unhappy. He enjoyed being a graphic artist and working with computers. What was wearing him down were the schedules and deadlines. He needed to take his basic skills and use them in a completely different environment, one in which he could do what he wanted in a way that honored his time and energy.

As a result of our conversation, he started traveling around the United States to find the place in which he could best live and work. It took him three months to decide to settle in Texas. Then he investigated how he could best adapt his skills to his new environment.

Today this person works with Native Americans, helping them to preserve their history and culture in computer art designs. His is a unique and special business that combines Indian knowledge and one person's skills.

This man is as happy as he can be. When he visited me recently, he told me his business is thriving. His pleased customers tell others of his work, and people from many walks of life ask him to make their ideas into artwork.

Money is no longer his main motive for working. He loves his new environment. He sets his own schedule and has more time for himself. I asked him how much money he needs and he told me he needs just enough to get by. He said, "I'm happy being out there with people and animals. I'm happy just talking, reading, giving time to myself. I never in my whole life lived this way. I get to do something creative and in the process help other people."

Look at your skills and talents. Are you using them? And if you are, are you using them in the environment that best suits your needs?

Where can you get support if everything else fails?

You want to make changes but are afraid that if you fail you won't have the support you need to survive. Realize that support exists. For instance, in addition to Alcoholics Anonymous and Overeaters Anonymous many other support groups assist people with just about every addiction and dysfunction there is. The easiest way is to start reading the Yellow Pages listings for health support groups—AA, OA, GA, etc.—then also contact local hospitals that have an outpatient support group. Every hospital has several. And these groups are found not just in cities, but in small towns throughout America. Although you don't necessarily have to use outside support, you should always be aware that it is available to you. It will help you to survive and get back on your feet in the worst-case scenario.

Keeping this in mind removes some of the pressure in your day-to-day existence. You have a backup plan to fall back on if all else fails. Otherwise, you'll always be tentative about taking any steps to make change happen.

Whom do you emulate?

Frequently, we emulate people beyond our class. That's why we're so preoccupied with people on soap operas and "Lifestyles of the Rich and Famous." We look up to these models even when we know we will never live like them.

What does that tell us? It says that we don't want to look at our own lives. We're afraid to acknowledge our own dreams and to actualize them. We simply accept other people's idea of how we should live if we had the resources. So we often end up living vicariously.

How does the struggle for security affect you?

Striving for security prevents you from taking chances. You're never willing to do anything you're not accustomed to because that would make you feel insecure.

I remember being interviewed on a television talk show by a physician and a reporter. The physician asked me, "Gary, what would you change about the American diet?" I said I would eliminate caffeine and sugar.

People called in from all over America and asked me what was left, to which I replied, "Are the only things in your life caffeine and sugar? There's so much more to life than what you eat and drink. You've got to realize that it is necessary to let go of the negative in order to create something positive." The physician later said to me, "People are just too lazy to change. They're just not going to do it."

It's true but it has more to do with insecurity than laziness. People feel so insecure that they won't even change the bad foods in their diet. They eat meals day after day that result in symptoms such as puffy eyes, indigestion, diarrhea, gas, and arthritic pains. But they won't give up the bad foods for a healthier diet because repeating habits they're used to makes them feel secure.

Are you prepared to make your life simpler?

What are you willing to do to make your life simpler? Take an inventory of the different areas of your life.

Relationships

Stop fighting. Stop trying to make relationships work. It's nonsense to work on another person's psyche, to mold and readjust your partner, to make compromises. If my feet are a size ten, I'm not going to wear a size six shoe and cripple myself in the process. A relationship either works or it doesn't.

When you're with someone you know if it feels right. If it doesn't, you need to look for someone else. It's that simple. There is no scarcity of people. Our ethic says, you made your bed, now lie in it. People think that because they've become involved with someone they've got to remain in the relationship for the rest of their lives no matter how good or bad the relationship is.

What happens when you adopt this attitude? Well, you may stay together and try to find ways to distract yourself from your unhappiness. One of you becomes alcoholic, the other becomes fat and depressed. You watch television and read the *National Enquirer.* You have an occasional affair and feel guilty about it. You're married and you feel bound by the law.

Why not feel good about being by yourself? Be free to explore life and the experiences you want. If you meet someone and it works out, fine. If it doesn't, that's fine also. No one is in the wrong. Let's stop blaming. Let's look at what's right.

There are no shortages of people to be happy with in this world. Somewhere out there are people who complement your personality. If you make your life uncomplicated and meet someone else who is uncomplicated, you'll have a basis for a good relationship.

Possessions

In order to make your life simpler, you've got to give things up. Make a list of what you're willing to give up to make your life less complicated. What do you own that you don't really use? Why not just give away the things in your life that you're not using? Give it away, throw it away, or use it. But stop cluttering. Clutter keeps you from being free.

What risks have you taken in each important area of your life?

Your growth is directly related to the challenges you give yourself. But challenges entail risk, and change, and you may be afraid of what those changes might mean. Maybe other people's attitudes toward you will change. Maybe your attitude toward other people will change. Maybe the circumstances of your existence will change. All of these possibilities may make you feel insecure, and if they do you may avoid risks at all costs.

An example of appropriate risks: Your schedule is very predictable? So, sit down and make up a brand new schedule where every hour will be done differently. Instead of TV and radio, go for a power walk or bike ride or go rollerblading. If you don't know how, you can get lessons.

At work, if a person gossips and it's bothering you, take a risk. Sit down privately. Are they aware of the effects of gossip on everyone, and how it affects you? You have no right to ask them to change their behavior to meet your needs. You do have the right to let that person know you don't like it and you won't accept it.

Instead of working over lunch, take your full lunchtime to go out each day and try a different type of food. Sit with people you don't know to try to create new friendships.

Instead of talking to friends and family about problems, have phone-free nights where you unplug the phone. Plan your evening in advance. One night a week, enjoy some cultural event—possibly a play, folk festival, orchestra, or cabaret. Plan a night of something—bowling or billiards—something out of character—pottery or glass blowing—become a Big Brother or Big Sister one night a week. In short, take some risks. These are minor things that break old habits and routines, and in turn enlarge life-enhancing perceptions and expand your reality base. This, in time, gives you confidence to take bigger risks, including career moves, possibly selling a home you're a prisoner to because of upkeep and maintenance, and how you may really want to see other places in American but can't afford to.

What can you depend upon?

In the world we live in, nothing is guaranteed. Human beings have trouble with this concept. The problem is, we don't like to think that something we consider permanent could be tenuous. Pink slips are handed daily to people who thought they had secure jobs. The biggest mistake most of these people have made is living beyond their means. The first thing they generally do upon being laid off is use their savings to maintain a stupid lifestyle they no longer need. Then they borrow from their friends and families and the bank. Now they're in debt.

Learning to be comfortable with less can ease much of the burden of life's stress. If you are laid off, get rid of everything and start over. Starting over is a whole new and exciting experience.

When I went to my high school reunion, many of my ex-classmates told me how their neighborhoods had changed for the worse. I asked why they didn't move and many replied that they couldn't leave because they had always lived in the same house or on the same street. It was home. They preferred to remain prisoners in their unsafe homes rather than give up the familiar.

Is any square footage worth your emotional health? It's just square footage. The energy that you have when you're there is what makes it special, and you can put out that same energy anywhere. You, and not the house, are the energy. But we give our homes a life of their own. We give them power that they shouldn't have. A house is an inanimate object that we make more powerful and controlling than it should be. We indebt ourselves to stone, brick, or wood. It's absurd when you think about it.

We need the willingness to let things go and say, thank you for allowing me to enjoy that when I did. Now it's time to move on.

Cultivating resourcefulness

Did you ever think about what you should have done but didn't? Have you thought about what opportunities you missed because of something you neglected to do?

Don't beat yourself up about what you didn't do. Learn from your mistakes. The next time an opportunity arises, be willing to take some risks. And if an opportunity isn't there, go out and make it happen. That's what people who succeed do.

The majority of people want someone to make their lives work for them. In the middle class, for instance, people are waiting for someone else to make things the way they used to be. They want to live like Ozzie and Harriet and the Cleavers did. They're waiting for the politicians to give them back safe neighborhoods. They're looking for government or industry to give them a secure job so that they can have a nice backyard with flowers and swings for the kids. They're waiting for someone to intervene and make it all nice again. But that will never happen.

It's fruitless to sit around and wait for someone to come and rescue you. You have to take whatever skills and assets you have, network with others, go to groups that support and strengthen you, and make life happen. You can either make your life work or become victimized.

Finding support

You can always find support for whatever it is you wish to do. I was talking with a man who has AIDS the other day. He said to me, "It's one thing for you to talk about eating right because you can afford to eat right, but not everyone can." I told him he was wrong. "I have not changed my standard of living in years," I said. "I live well within my financial means, but I deprive myself of nothing. I have what makes me happy. That enables me to take the extra money and work on the projects that I consider important." I went on to explain that I didn't spend a lot more money than he did on groceries. I sprout my own sprouts, which costs me about seven cents a day. This replaces more expensive and less nutritious store-bought foods.

Then I told him what he could do to eat better. "There's a house downtown that feeds about 1,600 to 1,800 persons with AIDS a month. You can get wonderful free meals made from organic food."

This man hadn't been aware of that. He was waiting for someone to come to him. But it doesn't work that way. You have to make the effort to help yourself. When you do, you will find that many wonderful connections exist. If you keep to yourself, you're not going to know about anything, and you'll remain helpless.

In almost every community in the country there are open centers. If you contact local health food stores or food co-ops, you can find a list of locations and dates of meetings. These will list dozens of self-help groups such as the Whole Foods Project in NYC. For a person who can't afford organic food from health food stores, there are organic co-ops, and every community has organic food outreach programs—just call local health food stores. There are regular health magazines for each area of the country. There are even those specific to individual cities. They list dozens of different health care providers, orthomolecular psychiatrists, homeopaths, chiropractors, nurse midwives, herbalists, psychologists, positive transpersonal explorations, meditation, yoga, cooking classes, etc. That is merely in the area of holistic health. There are also holistic career counselors to help with career changes.

Now this man has picked up my lead and found more than enough good food for himself. His possibilities have expanded because he made one phone call.

Once you stop feeling victimized by your circumstances,

you are free to make your life work. You're no longer waiting for someone to rescue you from bankruptcy, from a bad neighborhood, from a troubled school, or from any problems you might have. Make the breaks, and if you can't make them where you live, make them someplace else.

Bartering skills

Yes, you do need to be resourceful to ensure a better life where you can be free to do the things you want to do and to become the person you want to become. But cultivating resourcefulness can help you in every aspect of your life. Being resourceful simply means keeping yourself open to all your options. You may want to look at what you can share with someone else. If you put your ego aside, one person's skills combined with another's create a synergy that is greater than the simple sum of the individual efforts. Get small groups together and network. That's how things happen.

Something as simple as bartering can make a difference in your life. A friend of mine who was making $150 an hour lost his job and became sick and depressed. He was broke and couldn't find another job. He went to a food co-op and set up a computer system they needed. In exchange, he now gets organic food for free.

A lot of people don't feel comfortable with the idea of bartering. They're used to getting paid for what they do and don't know how to exchange services of equal value. You don't necessarily want to estimate the value of what you do according to its hourly worth in the consumer market. Decide, rather, on a value based upon what another person is exchanging with you, so that there is equality in the bartering. Let's say that you're a dentist and the person you're bartering with is a house cleaner. You would need to equate the service of the house cleaner with a particular aspect of what you are going to do to fix his teeth. That way you respect each other. As an example, let's say you want mercury fillings replaced with composites but you don't have the money. The dentist says the fee will be $5,000. The likelihood is that $500 is materials and $4,500 is fees to the doctor for labor. Let's say you're a school teacher and your time is worth one tenth of what the doctor's would be. So think of what you could offer someone that would establish a value for what you get. You're fluent in French so you offer the dentist French lessons in return for mercury removal. Since a French tutor makes more than a school teacher you'd charge sixty dollars per hour for tutoring—figuring it would take approximately fifty hours over a six month period to help the doctor. That's approximately one half but people in barter must adjust the value of what they're giving when giving their time. This is a human equation—it equalizes disparities between thirty dollars per hour and fifty dollars per hour so it's not a matter of working at your rate till you pay their rate—it's a common agreement that what you give of yourself is equal in effort what the other person is giving.

For example, someone wants to come to a two week health retreat which costs $2,500. The person is a dietician in a hospital and takes home $300 per week. Clearly it would take six months parttime work to make up the difference. That wouldn't be fair; so you select an amount of time that both people consider equitable—let's say fifty hours over a six month period. This way, she could work eight hours on Saturday and a few hours one or two evenings per week—it wouldn't upset her schedule and she'd be receiving a substantial discount, but there'd be some effort on her part in return, showing goodwill. In essence, bartering has as its basis a spiritual element—the desire to share but allow each person to give what they can, and then consider that equal. Otherwise, bartering benefits the person whose services are the most expensive, and that's neither fair nor the object of the exercise. After all, the most successful people understand the importance of compassion, which is the key element in the bartering process.

You'd be surprised how well bartering can work. A friend of mine knows a man who barters his paintings. In exchange he has gotten a yacht, a car, and free dental care. He's been to

Egypt where he has cruised down the Nile. This man lives off bartering. He's a smart individual who lives a very creative and carefree life filled with joy and love.

Do you go into debt to impress others?

Are you concerned about projecting a certain image? Do you buy clothes you can't afford or don't need just to be fashionable? Do you impress people with the size of your house? Do you feel you have to live in a certain neighborhood for reasons of status? Do you buy a thirty-thousand-dollar car when a thirteen-thousand-dollar vehicle is all you really need? Do you travel to where you want to go, or do you visit only fashionable places that will impress your friends?

So many people are wrapped up in maintaining an image. Recently I was working out in my health club with two people from my running group. The owner walked in and said, "We have rules in this building. Only two people in here at a time. There's also a dress code." I said, "We're wearing appropriate workout attire." (We had on shorts, tank tops, and tennis shoes.) He said, "It's a little Central Parkish. You look like you're running out there." I said, "No, we're in here working out." He said, "We like things that don't look so down there in the park." "In other words, I should wear a Calvin Klein top and Armani shorts?" "Yeah," he said, "something like that." I said, "Are you going to have fashion police come and arrest us if we don't dress right?"

When you think about where your money goes, you start to realize how many things, large and small, you do simply to project an image. Think about it: The purchase of many things in your life may have had nothing to do with making you happy.

Why not dress the way you want, live where you want, be with people you like to be with, and share in a relationship that is healthy and happy? Security isn't based on keeping the status quo and impressing those around you. True security lies in filling your waking moments with the activities that please you. When you make your choices from an inner peace, a calming effect comes over you. You are not allowing fear to lead you back into predictable self-defeating patterns. Finally, it's your life so try to honor it. Making positive choices and seeing the outcomes will only reaffirm security comes from making appropriate changes and having the confidence to stick with them.

Honoring Your Time

MOST OF OUR PROBLEMS AREN'T THE RESULT OF ONE ERROR. ONE-time mistakes are normal and natural, and you should allow yourself and others to make them. Likewise, you shouldn't be hard on yourself if you make errors in judgment; these are necessary if you are to grow. It's the pattern of repeated mistakes that can lead you astray.

My years of counseling have shown me that most problems do not stem from whether a person is good or bad, or positive or negative. They stem from making the wrong decisions, trying to honor the wrong self. The key is to know yourself and your needs. If you don't how can you make the right choices to honor those needs?

Describe yourself. That's the first crucial step in examining whether you honor your time.

To what do you give quality time or attention?

You are going to be giving your life to something. The question is, to what? To what are you really dedicating your twenty-four hours each day? To a certain lifestyle? To the manifestation of ego and image? To a higher ideal? To scholarship? What are you becoming? When you're a child you can't wait until you get big enough to turn the doorknobs and wash your hands in the sink, or until you can drive a car. You look forward to what you're becoming. When you're going through high school and college you are becoming something.

Once you get out into the world, do you suddenly feel as though it's too late to become something? It's not too late. You're going to place attention on something; what will it be? Are you honoring your work, your life beyond your work, your family? Do you have to pay attention to family needs? What are their real needs versus their superficial needs? How much attention are you giving to those real needs? Or *are* you giving any attention to them?

Your needs versus family responsibilities

If yours is like many American families, everyone will be doing whatever they're going to do on their own to create their own identities, and while they'll be sharing a common space for a period of time, there won't be a whole lot of quality communication. (That's one of the reasons why grandparents in other cultures are valuable to the family. They act as the communicators for the unresolved conflicts between children and their parents. There is generally no threat from the grandparents. Rather, there's a sense of trust and patience. They're willing to forgive. They're not apt to chastise or criticize. They're looking to be the bridge.)

You've got time each day. If you don't focus attention on that time, it will be meaningless. At the end of each day, it's another day out of your life. And you will not be able to live that day again. If you're trying to do something with that time that doesn't honor the real needs of the real self, then it's wasted time. Why not put that time into focus?

This is a workbook, and, of necessity, it's advocating working in the present because, after all, you can't work in the past. So forget the past. Do not let the past dictate that you're not good enough or not smart enough or not lovable enough or not complete enough. It's important for you to start over today. Start the game over. If this means leaving a job, leaving an area, or deciding to put time into this instead of that, then this is what you are going to do. But you are not going to change out of anxiety or haste. The whole idea is to prepare so that when you do make the change it is not superficial and you have the strength to follow through.

Recently I counseled a married couple that spend no time together. I suggested a few things they could do together each day. One suggestion was to go out and befriend a homeless person each day, talk with him or her, and give the person some food. They started going out together and found this to be one of the most rewarding parts of their day. They started seeing homeless people as human beings, not just as people they wished were in someone else's neighborhood.

How many hours a day do you waste by giving time to people who don't appreciate it? Be careful not to give your time to someone who abuses you. If all your time with someone is spent listening to him talk about himself, what's the point of being with that person? The person doesn't care about you. If you stop frittering away your time on that person and placing it where it does count, you'll be doing yourself a favor.

I'm not saying you shouldn't give time to people who are seeking your counsel. Of course you'll want to do that occasionally. But you need to cut loose the people who come back repeatedly with the same problems but never do anything with your advice. While anyone can have a problem and want —and legitimately need—to talk about it, you have to learn to recognize the pattern of people who drain you or who always take but don't return the support. There comes a day when you have to say to these people, I've listened, I've been understanding, I've given you my suggestions. Please either take my suggestions, show me where they aren't usable, or don't complain anymore.

Often their reaction to this is hostile. They're likely to call you insensitive and cold. Suddenly, it's all your fault. You became a target for their anger because you caught them in their act. It's like catching a liar in a lie; watch how quickly they blow their cool. People who are caught in something dishonest will overreact; the whole idea of overreacting is to make you feel guilty for having caught them. But you don't have to feel guilty. Say, "Yell at the wind. I'm out of here." You'll save yourself a lot of time.

It comes down to this: For every person you help who doesn't want or respect that help, you're keeping your attention from a person who would accept your help and become a stronger person for it. It's like feeding a fat person who is moaning because they haven't had a meal in the past two hours instead of giving the food to a person who is starving to death. There's a limit to what we're capable of giving. So don't be afraid to qualify what you're giving. You have the right to do that. Sometimes guilt keeps us from doing that, but you have to get beyond guilt.

Give your time to people who respect you for it. You'll know intuitively that something good is coming from it. There's a bond that develops between people. You'll feel it.

One more thing on the subject of helping others: There's a big difference between helping people for the right reasons and using the act of helping as an excuse to hide your own inefficiency at living by acting as if you're some sort of saint or martyr. People can get caught up in what I call the wounded ego syndrome. They've been hurt and made to feel worthless. They have taken this seriously and now all they do is immerse themselves in other people's problems, hoping that everyone will think they're a nice person. They're always helping and never have a moment for themselves. This is not healthy.

Do the things you do feel natural and honest?

I know a man who two years ago was in crisis. He had a successful practice in corporate law but found that his clients were not ethical people. He felt trapped by compromises he had to make in order to protect their interests. Although he was well paid and only doing what every other lawyer did, he could not respect his own decisions. He realized that he'd been considering his income first, rather than his decisions. As a result, he woke up one day and concluded that he couldn't live this lie anymore. His work was dishonest.

Now the things he does are honest and natural. He's left law altogether. He works in a northern California spa showing people how to take care of themselves. He gave up the $300,000 a year and the high-class lifestyle to live in an adobe hut. It doesn't make sense to others, but it does to him. That's because he's being honest and doing what's natural. He feels great working with people without having to compete against them. He doesn't have to be mercenary and hurt people. He's happy.

Unfortunately his family is not happy with his version of success. Can you imagine a family saying you're wrong for being happy because the way you're doing it doesn't make us happy? His father, who is also an attorney, has been angry ever since he made the change. He won't talk to his son; he just yells at him. But then his father never talked with him anyway. He *always* yelled at him. The mother would not interfere with the father, who was a very dominant man.

It was easy to see how my buddy got caught up in believing that he had to prove himself by being a tough corporate lawyer, making money, and being successful. He was saying, "Hey dad, have I done enough to get a hug?" But he could never do enough. When you're insecure, there is never enough.

Now he's a different human being. He looks ten years younger. His body is different. He used to run to win. Now he runs because he likes to run.

What drives you?

Our passions are what drives us. That is, assuming we allow ourselves to express or experience passion. If, for example, you want to learn a particular craft and you spend the required time, studying and apprenticing to master your craft, and then one day someone asks you, what motivates or drives you to give this type of commitment to this craft, what is your answer? If it is because you simply enjoy it or you feel good doing it, that's fine. If, however, you are doing it to prove to someone that you deserve respect or attention, or that you love them, your drive is motivated by a need for self-validation. So ask yourself what drives you. What do you expect to get from your efforts?

How do you spend time alone?

How do you feel about spending time alone? Your attitude determines whether that time is constructive, positive, and invigorating, or depressing, anxiety-provoking, and lonely. If you adopt the first attitude your life is in greater balance than if you hold the second view.

When you feel good about spending time alone you can use that time to read, create, study, focus, clear out, unclutter, and set new priorities. But if you feel anxious about being alone, you end up squandering your time. You keep the television or radio on or spend too much time on the telephone to keep feelings of loneliness at bay. Your precious time becomes wasted.

How do you sublimate?

Determining the ways that you sublimate will identify the parts of your life you're not honest with and not finding fulfillment in. What are the most common ways men sublimate? Sports are important for a man. Football, baseball, and basketball are the most popular sports for men, and what do all of these have in common? They're team sports. Men love the fellowship of other men.

But as things work out in our culture, once you become a family man you lose the comfort of other men. That's one of the tragedies of our society. One of the biggest mistakes the institution of marriage has ever created is the demand for full time and attention. I can't tell you how many men get married and then can no longer retain their best friends. They never seem to have the time to get together with them. Or they do have the time but there's the thought that the friendship is competitive with the marriage, especially if the friend is a single man.

There should be no reason for that. If a person is a friend, he should always be a friend, and you should make time in your life for friends. A very important part of being balanced and healthy is to have quality relationships with men and women. I do not believe in monogamy as we now know it. I'm not referring to sexual monogamy, but rather to an exclusivity of time and attention. It's unnatural. Many crises in marriages and relationships are the result of one person trying to be all things to another person. The woman tries to become the mother, the mistress, the soothsayer, and all other things, when it's not possible. Similarly, a man cannot be all things to a woman. Why can't people be smart enough to realize this?

For a man, the loss of meaningful friendships is terrible to his sense of self-esteem. There's a betrayal of the masculine bonds that historically have kept men together. That's why sports, even though they may seem barbaric, are ways men identify what is uniquely masculine in the effort to pursue a state of excellence. Men identify and feel like they're one of the team; that's why men adopt a team. That adoption becomes a part of the extended male family. When men take time on a Sunday afternoon to watch a ball game, they're not just watching a sport to distract themselves and waste three or four hours. They're continuing a bond that identifies what is uniquely masculine and lonely in them. They are showing that they're still connected.

Everyone needs more than one person in his or her life to communicate with. You need a variety of people with which you can share multiple ideas and multiple energies because you have multiple energies to share. So regardless of whether you're married or not, you should establish what kinds of friends you need. Ask yourself, what do you want to share with your friends? If you don't do that, then the part of you that seeks friendship has to sublimate. It has to go somewhere. Unresolved energy must find an outlet, and it always will. Whether it's a disease process, or a manic process, or something constructive, an outlet will emerge. Your outlet might be, for example, compulsive work, so that you end up having no time for yourself.

If you are married, ask yourself whether you are honoring the institution of marriage, or perhaps an unquestioned and old conception of it, instead of being spontaneous and honest and honoring what is natural. Institutional beliefs tend not to be natural; after all, the whole idea of an institutional belief is that the institution is controlling us. Ironically, the institution can become like a service industry. The institution services our dysfunction. And what is the cause of our dysfunction? Not being happy with how we feel in the institution!

Sometimes our whole behavior gets bound up in negative patterns instead of positive ones. This is what happens in sublimation. Overeating, taking drugs, smoking, and working compulsively are all ways of sublimating.

A healthier idea is to ask yourself, what are you really missing in life, and how could that need be met if it weren't being sublimated?

Describe how you honor what you value

How do you honor those things that matter to you? For example, I honor health every day by getting up and doing something good for my body. My diet and my mind and my exercise honor my body because I value it. Likewise, if I value my friendships I honor those by engaging in them in the best ways I know how. I don't engage in anything that would destroy the friendships or dishonor the personhood of my friends—that is, that would infringe upon the sanctity of their inner beings. This may sound simple, but it pays to remember that your friend is first and foremost a person, not just a friend. In other words, I can't assume that because a person is my friend I have the right to say anything. I can't just show up at my friend's house and assume that because he's my friend he has no boundaries. On the contrary, by honoring his boundaries, I am honoring his personhood and thus the friendship.

If I value creativity then every day I'll set aside time to create, even if only an hour. I'll make that time. And for whatever else I value, I'll make more time. Of course that means I will not put time and attention into things I do not value. If you ask me to do something I do not value, I won't do it. Those are the choices that make a difference in how I define my life.

Ask yourself what you value. Then ask what you do to show it.

When you work hard, what do you really want?

What are you really looking for from all that hard work? You may be looking for satisfaction, pleasure, and finally recognition. But if you're *only* looking for recognition, something's wrong.

Do something you really like and you won't need recognition from it. Do you ever notice how many times an artist will work on a piece of work, no matter what it is. It isn't for the public. It's for herself. It doesn't matter if it's never shown, never sold. She does it for herself, to honor her inner spirit.

This idea can be applied to any area of endeavor. If you're living a life in which you're paying attention to what honors your inner needs, then you don't really require recognition. The public is of no consequence, because the doing itself is the recognition. You feel good about every moment so you don't have to say, can I have some recognition now? Did I do what I was supposed to do?

Stop and think about how many times you did something for other people because you needed the recognition in return.

You had a hidden agenda, and thus the time and energy you spent on what you were doing was not honestly spent. The problem is, without honesty there is no effortlessness, nothing natural; everything is manipulation. What you are doing is putting a lot of intense energy into something that ultimately imbalances you.

Natural processes keep you balanced and focused. They keep you going in one direction, and something positive will come from that.

One more thing: In the normal course of life, you *will* get a response from the decent people around you. It is natural to respond. I respond to things people do that I consider special; I'll always acknowledge them. Most people are going to do the same thing. The point is, if you find that you absolutely need that reinforcement in order to keep doing what you're doing, then you have to ask yourself whether you're working hard on the wrong things.

Where do you need to organize?

Do you need to organize in discipline, focus, or attention? Take a total inventory of yourself. As part of that, each week ask yourself "what have I done?" If you haven't done anything worth noting, you're obviously not willing to take control of your life. You're still waiting for someone to fill in the blanks. There was a time, by the way, when I would do that. I would fill in all your blanks for you. I'd tell you how to get discipline and I'd tell you about your fears. Well, I didn't help anyone. I was trying to take on something that people had to do for themselves.

It's your life. You've got to not only fill in the blanks but also create the blanks to fill in! That's because you don't learn primarily from the quality of your answers, you also learn from the quality of your questions. There's far more profundity in the question than there is in the answer. So you have to figure out the best way to ask the questions. Once you do, you're on the right track.

A simple organizational chart might assist you in better managing your time and projects:

Date
Time—over the next 12 months
Project—sell everything I don't need
Goal—get out of debt
Short term
    (a) get estimates of current market values
    (b) get rental rates for comparable space
    (c) hire a specialty broker
Research
    1. estimate current income, saving, expenses
    2. what are my buying habits
    3. what do I own that I don't use, like, or need
    4. how much more would I save if I stopped buying stuff and sold what I don't need
    5. where would I like to live
    6. how would I like to live
    7. how much time do I spend working to pay down my debt
    8. what would I do with the extra free time
    9. how well do I manage the stresses caused by my standard of living
    10. do I need help doing any part of this
    11. list the support groups that I could go to

After reviewing your chart, you may change your priorities, but at least you know where you are headed and how you are going to get there. Or if you need focus and attention, there are Buddhist classes that are phenomenal for getting focus. Just look in the phone book under Buddhist.

There's always a resource to help you if you are at least honest in knowing what you need help with. It's not necessary that you do it all yourself if you have others who can help guide you into change. Combine your energy with other people to mutually enhance all of your lives.

What is divine within you?

Define that which is divine or the eternal spirit within you. Then you can honor it. We can get very caustic and very down on ourselves, and as a result we forget that we are divine beings filled with a divine energy. You are that energy. What are you going to do with it? How are you going to nourish it and manifest it? One thing that almost everyone has experienced is being around people who manifest their divine energy; there's a comfort and joy in just occupying the same space.

You can become the person that gives comfort and joy to other people because you will be able to provide this energy simply by manifesting it in yourself.

I feel that everyone has enormous reservoirs of passion for life that just remain locked inside them. It's as if people have a lush oasis within them but instead of tapping into it most wander through the desert of trying to live their lives based on the wrong premise. Use all the wonderful energy inside you instead of reverting to blaming, anger, disappointments, sublimations, and dysfunction. Just let go of the negative so you can find what works, and realize what is divine.

What was missing when you've felt bad?

Frequently I find it helpful to ask questions that are the opposites, or the negatives, if you will, of what one would normally ask. Thus, if someone comes to me and says, "I feel bad," I don't say, "What made you feel bad?", but rather, "What wasn't there?" Their response is often the quickest answer that will give them the truest insight. What wasn't there is what they weren't working on, what they didn't pay attention to but perhaps should have.

So when you feel bad, something is missing. What is it? Otherwise, when you feel bad, what do you feel? You feel sadness and despair. You feel those because something isn't there.

An example. You knew someone was stealing at work. Everyone else knew also, but kept quiet. You first confronted the person who was stealing and told them to stop or go elsewhere. They told you to mind your own business, so you told the owner. The other workers were angry at you. So for honoring your ethics, you did the right thing, even if others didn't like you for doing it.

If you've ever felt good about a particular situation but were conditioned to feel bad about it, you have to make the choice about which attitude to trust. Can you trust yourself to create answers and solutions even if you were taught that when something bad happens you just have to accept it? People get into this self-deprivation and self-destructive pattern instead of saying, I feel bad because I'm lacking something. I'm going to look for what I need to feel good and I'm going to find it or create it.

Do you judge yourself by what's in your heart and mind?

In most cases you judge yourself by your accomplishments. It's easier and usually what you were taught to do. But in doing so, you lose focus of the inner self.

Few people learn what it means to feel something from the heart or from their inner being. We're taught to focus on external factors, and these become the all-important feature of life. But if you get caught up in judging your life by your experiences, you'll start to constantly anticipate the next experience. That, in turn, is going to make you think about the consequences of the experience, as opposed to just experiencing it. So the sense of dread, loss of control, or fear of something negative happening can take over.

Do you find that long periods of your life are simply wasted waiting for an experience to happen? You wait for the good experience that you feel will redeem the time you have been in the limbo of waiting. You get overly focused on what is mundane when you keep on this experience-seeking path that has no purpose and no end.

What areas of free will and freedom do you use?

How do you use freedom? Make a list.

1. to be your own person
2. to take responsibility for your own actions
3. to actively seek the right goals for your true inner needs
4. to let negative people know that you won't accept negative energy
5. to commit yourself to causes that make you feel good
   a. environmental actions groups
   b. men or women's study groups
   c. adult education classes to broaden your knowledge
   d. political and religious action groups
6. to unclutter your life—give it away, throw it away, or use it wisely
7. to organize your time so you count
8. to let go of unnecessary responsibilities

This very important exercise will tell you an awful lot about yourself. For instance, when is the last time you did something completely out of character, spontaneous, and different from what anyone would expect from you? It was probably a really long time ago. Why? When did you use freedom last and how did you use it? If you don't use the freedom you have, it's like muscle tissue that turns to fat.

The whole idea of being free is to express what's in our hearts and minds. Of course with freedom comes a responsibility to not abuse others. With that in mind, if you're not afraid of what's in your heart, then you will find other people who will acknowledge that and honor it as well. I've never found a situation where I couldn't find someone who was interested in freedom and who would be interested in what I am. When two people share an understanding of their own freedom, you have endless ways of demonstrating that freedom. The people who are afraid of freedom within themselves are the people who are invulnerable. You can know them for a hundred years and never know them because they're never going to reveal what's really inside.

What are you doing with freedom? How have you expressed it? How have you used it? How are you making it work for you?

I talk a lot with cab drivers who tell me that in their native countries people don't have any right to freedom. They can't express their feelings, emotions, political views, sexual views, religious views, creative views. They don't have any of this. And here so many of us just abuse freedom. We think freedom is just an opportunity for gluttony or for being a loudmouth or for being selfish. How sad that more Americans don't use freedom in a constructive way to help society and to experience growth in the process.

Write down the ways you use your freedom.

Can you live with uncertainty?

Uncertainty creates fear, which limits free will. As long as you're uncertain about who you are, what you want, and what you need to get what you want, the uncertainty becomes that big bugaboo that stands right in front of you. Perhaps every day you get up to do something and you're uncertain. I don't know if I should go back to school. ... I don't know if I should move to San Diego. ... I don't know if I should change my diet. ... People are very confused in our society; they're uncertain of everything. And they don't like it.

But is cast-in-stone certainty really an asset in life? The need for constant certainty means that you will never change. Why do you think conservatives are so conservative? They have something to conserve! People who are in positions of power need certainty in all things because they don't want to change. They can't have a society where people express themselves openly and freely. They can't have people manifesting change because then they would lose control and power.

Here are some examples of a counterproductive need for certainty: When you have to find a friend that's good before you'll drop the "friend" you don't really like. When you have to develop a relationship that's better before you'll get out of a bad relationship. When you have to have a body you really like before you'll start exercising. You end up defeating yourself in each case.

People don't change in any area of their life unless they have confidence that the change is going to be beneficial. This makes sense. The problem comes when they're not willing to let go of anything—even the bad things—and replace them with something unless they're certain of success. So they start looking for input that allows them to feel some certainty that the change is going to work, some certainty that the business is going to work or that the relationship will, or the job, or the career, or the move, or whatever the change is. The trouble is, nothing in life is certain.

The need for certainty breeds a contempt for uncertainty, yet it's only with uncertainty that we can change. Learn to be confident with uncertainty. Learn to feel the discomfort that accompanies change without focusing on it and that discomfort will disappear. This will allow you the flexibility and freedom to be yourself and take the consequences of whatever happens. When a person is healthy and balanced, she or he will take whatever doesn't work and simply say, it's okay. Nothing in life is meant to work all the time. I took a chance and tried; it didn't work; I'll try something else. Healthy people, and people who are kind to themselves, are not afraid of uncertainty. They make it work for them, and—here is the key —they learn from it.

Feeling Passion and Desire

At some point in your life you finally decide to get out of your own way and go after what you want. You begin knowing what is important to you. Yesterday no longer exists, you've let it go. You've realized that what it takes to survive is an adaptive mind; the nonadaptive mind stagnates trying to honor allegiances to things it was taught to accept in the past, and you don't choose stagnation.

Now you've got a whole new mindset that you're learning to take control of and you want to move with it. You want to do something with all this insight, energy, and power.

Even now, though, when you start to do something, you may get in your own way by saying to yourself, "Hold on, I don't know if I can handle this. I'm not sure I really want to redirect my life. I've been this way for so long that I'm used to things as they are. I'm used to this kind of mess in my life. I'm used to the excuses I give. I'm used to the patterns of emotional malfeasance that I indulge in." When this happens, don't wait for the old self to react. It will just stand there and say, "I don't know." What kind of option is that?

The new side of you says, "I don't want to argue with anyone, least of all myself. What's the point? I'm going to examine the consequences of my actions. If I get up and exercise, then my metabolism is going to improve. If I go out and look for new ways to share my energy, then I'll stop repeating old patterns. I know what it feels like to be stuck in the same old place, and I'm tired of it." When you hit a barrier, the new side of you will say, "Take a break. Go to the beach, hang out,

117

and then come back and start over." The new self seeks positive change. It won't let other people influence or stop those changes.

When it's time to start organizing your life, start with minigoals that take a week or two to achieve. Tie several together to form larger goals. Take your ideals, ambitions, and dreams; pull them together to consolidate them into the strength you need.

When you set larger goals, you don't necessarily have to see the end product; goals can just be formulated as the things you want to change without a final solution. Maybe your goal is to live someplace else in a year's time. You don't have to know where that someplace is, but you can use your time to explore until you find a place that feels right. It's a world of adventure; life should be fun. Instead of concerning yourself with what you're trying to secure, focus on creating balance. You should find nice people and opportunity everywhere. If not, you can make that another goal.

So often people fight change merely to protect their egos or to cover up insecurity. But as the saying goes, "The wise water moves around the rock." It doesn't go up against it and become stagnant. Set a year or six months' goal for yourself, asking, "Can I be the person in that period of time who will have the competence and inner resources to take control of my life?" When you hit a barrier, you're immediately going to think of several options to get around it. In my opinion, you need to have five options for fluidity in any situation. If you start thinking of options, you will create alternatives.

How do you share your special qualities?

Do you share different parts of yourself with different people? Perhaps as a child you learned to clown around at home and make people laugh. Although you're still able to amuse your friends, you close yourself off to having fun at work. You think a serious image is needed at all times to gain the trust and respect of others. As a result, you cut off an important side of yourself.

Notice where you feel safe and where you don't. Maybe life taught you that being yourself in the professional world makes you vulnerable and easy prey for others who are looking for an opportunity to knock you down so that they can get ahead. Unfortunately, this is an overly competitive world, and you may tend to fear that others will take advantage of your openness and use that against you. So the things you would like to say are kept inside. You say only what you believe others are going to accept. Although you may be protecting yourself in this way, you're also denying an important part of your nature.

What if you had just one personality all the time? Think of how simple your life could be. Other people could accept or reject you for what you are and you wouldn't need to constantly adjust what you say and do just to please them. Some people would hate you for it, but you'd learn from that to weed them out of your life.

I would rather have no friends than to have false friends. I would rather have intelligent, sensitive conversations with myself than with a bunch of bubbleheads that I'm trying to somehow placate. I would rather have the connection with my own heart than with cold, embittered hearts. What is the purpose of cluttering up your life with people you can't communicate with honestly and compassionately?

Ask yourself, how much of your real self do you actually share? Do you share your essential nature or a manufactured, contrived personality? Do you share some of both, depending upon whom you feel safe with?

When you love yourself first, you share your life only with others who treat you lovingly. Whatever you are is enough. You don't have to be two, three, or five different people. You don't have to placate others' insecurities and prejudices. Nor do you have to honor their belief systems when they don't represent how you feel. You are able to communicate your real needs to friends by clearly defining what their friendship means to you.

If a person is intimidated by your honesty he or she might think, "Are you telling me that if I ask you something you're just going to say what you feel? That's scary. I don't want to hear what you really have to say. I want to be around people who give me a false sense of being okay because I'm insecure about myself. I want you there as a false sounding board. You're my psychoanalyst for free. I want us to spend twenty years together sharing the same nonsense. You're telling me that you're going to be honest with me and going to share love, but I wouldn't know love if I saw it because I was never given love, only conditional responses. If I did well I was given a reward. If I didn't I was punished. I'm a product of all that and I use it as an excuse not to change my life. Therefore, I surround myself with people who dislike me. You're telling me you're going to be different—the one person in my life who's going to be radiant, joyful, and always happy. I can't handle that." And that's how it often works.

Conversation, which ought to express your true beliefs, is easy when you're not worried about what the other person thinks of you. If that person isn't looking for the kind of friendship you have to offer, so be it. There are enough healthy, balanced, joyful people out there wanting a friendship based on truth.

Notice your special qualities by looking at different areas of your life. What have you done to make different parts of your life work? What parts of your life don't work because you have neglected them? Ask yourself, "How can I apply my special qualities to these areas of my life?" Determine where you are able to share wit, charm, compassion, insight, wisdom, selflessness, courage, and trustworthiness.

Can you accept another person as he or she is?

People usually have certain qualities that you can relate to and others that you cannot. Does this mean you have to accept someone totally or avoid the person altogether? Not necessarily.

Few people will agree with you on every issue. If the differences between you and someone else are not interfering with your peace of mind, you can still enjoy being with that person. As long as the person does not in any way undermine who you are, you have the basis for a relationship. I might have friends with different political philosophies. One might be a communist, another a capitalist, and the third a socialist. It is our ability to respect each other as people—and not our politics—that is going to determine the quality of our friendship.

Look at your relationships to see whether your differences are frustrating the affiliation or not. Are you comfortable around the other person or do his or her beliefs make you uneasy? If they make you uncomfortable, you need to draw the line and reconsider the relationship.

Are you giving mixed messages?

You may be in a relationship where you want to share something with the other person but you don't know how. You're afraid that your passion and desire are more than the person can bear. You're terrified of being rejected. As a result, you end up never really feeling completely fulfilled with the person.

The other person may have the same thoughts and may also be afraid to impose them on you. Both of you are frustrated. Your relationship becomes superficial.

Relationships become meaningful when both people's desires are met. You should be able to tell a person what you're thinking right up front.

We're a society that fears being honest about our passions and desires. Partly it's because people tend to gossip, which makes it hard to confide our innermost thoughts. In the back of our minds we wonder, who else is going to know about this?

You've got to let the person know that what you're sharing with him or her is only meant for that person. You're not sharing this with their girlfriends, boyfriends, mother, father, or work associates. You don't want what you share to be the topic of discussion. Let the person agree to honor that privacy before you share anything at all.

A person who betrays your confidence is not a person you should have in your life. Yet the reality is that a lot of people out there will betray you at the drop of a hat. Somehow we've forgotten about trust and honor. We seem to have become motivated by fear and by the desire to satisfy immediate needs, which has led us to a largely mercenary attitude, with our own interests superseding those of others, or the community. We should often give pause to reflect: What are my actions, thoughts, and deeds going to mean to those around me? But we don't do this which makes us a dysfunctional nation, at least ethically.

Are you able to share confidences with anyone? If not, is it because you don't trust the people in your life? Are you a trustworthy person yourself?

Make a list of the things you wanted to do but. . . .

Make a list of things you wanted to do but never did. Choose one item from your list and create a program to make it happen. Maybe you wanted to be a ballerina but. . . . It doesn't matter that you're not going to be performing at the Met. You can become a ballerina in your dance class. Give yourself time to make it happen, even if it takes a year or more.

Whatever you want to do, there is a way to make it work.

There are support groups, adult education courses, books, everything you need to bring your dream to fruition. Right now, in New York City, there are hundreds of study groups, classes, and social groups of all types. Every one of these groups started with one person saying, "I'm not going to say, 'I wanted to but ... ,' I'm going to make it happen."

I know a man named Rupert Ravens. At one point in his life he was a drug addict and an alcoholic who was wasting a great young life. He had been a top athlete in high school and then he postponed his life for about 15 years while he engaged in addictive behaviors. He was working as a house painter to make a living, although he was a very gifted artist, and the fumes were racking his body and affecting his immune system. The first step he chose to change his life was to detoxify his body.

One day he said to me, "Gary, I don't have any money. I can't buy vitamins or even organic produce. And I hate the idea of eating pesticide-contaminated produce." I suggested that he call some suppliers and start a food co-op. That way he would be able to get food at cost.

He got a group of people together and started a food co-op. They were able to buy produce at a fifty-percent saving, (cheaper than buying food in a supermarket). Instead of being helpless and not having the money to buy food, Rupert buys more healthy food at a lower price.

His confidence has reached new heights. The co-op has 100 members and is on the way to becoming one of the largest in New Jersey. It has more organic produce than any health food store in New York City. What's more, in a period of four weeks Rupert formed art classes and health support groups to encourage other people, including a running and walking club in southern New Jersey. These things benefit and honor Rupert's community but he is helping himself in the process by honoring his spiritual self.

I'd say that's pretty good for four weeks. If he can do it, why couldn't you? Why couldn't anyone? He could just as easily have hung around bars for the rest of his life, but he chose instead to self-actualize. He chose to enhance the best that he is instead of condemning himself for what he is not.

All this is the result of one man deciding to do exactly what I'm asking you do to. Make a list of all the things you wanted to do but. ... Then create the reality. Fill in the blanks in your life. Work alone or find other people who share your goal. When two, three, four, or more people have common goals, think of how much good they can do. Perhaps you have a talent and someone else has the money. Why not get together and make things happen even faster than they would if you worked separately? As long as there's a basic sense of trust between you, you can make it work.

Where do you turn for solutions to your problems?

You've started on your journey by analyzing who you are and noting your positive and negative qualities. You've begun the process of preparation and have created the hero within. You're inner-directed, self-empowered, and all set to change.

To whom do you turn for help in this effort? Who will help you with your creative, emotional, spiritual, mental, and physical challenges? And are the people you turn to in fact providing you with the right catalysts? Consider whom you turn to when faced with each of these challenges.

Creative challenges

If I want to do something creative, whom do I seek out for support? Creative people. Look for people who have succeeded at what you're attempting to do. An uncreative person has no framework. If you're interested in learning about medicinal herbs, you're not going to ask an orthodox doctor who doesn't even know what an herb is. He won't understand herbs because he has no background in them. You go to a holistic doctor who has been using herbs for years, because she or he will be able to help you.

When you find a person whose life is working, don't be afraid to ask that person for help. The most selfless people, the ones always giving of their energy, are the ones doing the most. It's easy to do more when your life works. The person whose life doesn't work is the one who is bitter and not willing to spend time with you.

Spiritual challenges

Who are the people best able to help you with spiritual issues? Look within yourself, not out there. All the answers you need are within you. You can touch the spirit when you let go of fear and you let go of the material.

People spend their whole lives looking for spiritual help by running to evangelists or gurus. We try strange ways to connect with our inner self. We go everywhere but inside.

Why not look inside? Why not trust what's in there? One explanation might be that in your life you've never been allowed to be the authority. Authority, you learned, comes from somewhere else. You, like most people, don't have either power or control. But if you understand that all you need to know is within, you will spend time sitting in quiet contemplation to find the answers.

You've been taught, however, to seek out experts, such as psychiatrists and other doctors, or priests, rabbis, or lawyers. But why is everyone an expert about your life except you?

Beware: Experts can take control of your life and negate your intuition. A doctor might say, for example, that you must have a radical mastectomy. You respond by saying that you were under the impression that a simple lumpectomy is a safer, more effective option. The doctor, in turn, will negate your knowledge by replying, "When did you get your medical degree? Where do you come off challenging me? Nobody does that. I have to dismiss you for being a bad patient." But you're not a bad patient, just an empowered one. The difficulty is in trying to talk with someone in power about anything that challenges that power. It causes a reaction that is not necessarily based on reason.

When you look at spiritual, as well as emotional, mental, and physical areas of your life, often you're your own best teacher.

List new possibilities

Look at the possibilities in different avenues of life. Look at all the possibilities that exist for each of these factions of your life.

For yourself

What possibilities can you see for yourself? What would you like to make happen? Make a chart and map it out. If you want to move to a new location, place that at the center of your chart. Then write your reasons for moving around it. Perhaps you want less clutter and responsibility. That will tell you that you're now in a place where there is too much clutter and responsibility. You might feel the need to start unloading your possessions.

Then you can start taking action. After deciding what things you no longer need, you can start the process of disengagement by bagging or boxing things and giving them away. In a short time you will have the freedom you desire and moving will be easy.

You can decide where it is best for you to live by listening to your heart. Visiting possible new locales will give you a feeling for what different places are like. For instance, in Boulder, Colorado, you might find intellectual energy and beautiful surroundings. New York might attract you if you plan to advance your career. If you're an artist you might enjoy living around Taos or Santa Fe. If you want to live quietly you might enjoy Tucson. If you want a combination of culture and ambience, you can go to Dallas. If you want to be where people are laid back and having fun with life, you can go to San Diego. If you want to be a part of a close community with intense intellectual activity, you might decide to live in San Francisco. If you want to be where people are more adventurous and poetic you can live in Portland. Find the place that feels comfortable, where you can meet people like yourself. Once you make the move, you will find it easier to make your life work.

For your family

Define possibilities for your family. That might include new ways of relating, connecting, healing old wounds, and communicating. It might mean having more time for your children.

In your marriage or your primary relationship, it might mean recapturing the romance you once felt. Go back and remember the passion and excitement of your romance when you were captivated by each other and joyful just being together. Having fun, as opposed to materialistic concerns, was all-important. If you could do it all over again, would you choose to have all the things you've accumulated, or quality time to share your passion?

One time through is all you get. Think of that when you create new possibilities for yourself, your children, and your relationships; it may impel you to change your priorities. You may want to replace false responsibilities in your life with possibilities built around love.

For your friends

What are some new possibilities with friends? Making new friends might be one. What qualities would you look for in new friends? They might have similar interests, enabling you to do things together. They might be people who love you for being you. They might have positive attitudes and compassionate hearts.

They will not be people who undermine, criticize, and talk about you behind your back.

For your work

What new possibilities can you envision at work? How about creating your own ideal job? Self-employment is an exciting, exhilarating experience. But what about sharing your business dreams with other people who have similar desires? Working together can create a synergy; a lot more happens when two or three people are working together. You can do it on your own—many people have—but it's a lot of more fun and a lot more efficient to work with other people that you trust. When each person helps out and there's no selfishness, everyone's needs can be met.

For society

What are some new possibilities for society? As a part of society, you need to involve yourself with it. There are a lot of members of the baby boom generation who don't do a thing for society; they're too busy focusing on themselves. I can't imagine being in a society and not contributing to it.

You could choose to make one day a week available to helping some segment of society. As an example, you can give one day a week pro bono, based upon your profession. If you're an attorney or an architect, you can donate time to any number of church centers that fund charities for the homeless. Or you could become a Big Brother or Big Sister to one of the six million orphaned children in America. You can also donate time to the local school system or to other public causes. Commit to making it work, just as you do on a personal level.

For *nature*

What possibilities allow you to reconnect with nature? Everybody loves nature if given the opportunity to experience it; I always notice how, when people come down to my ranch, they spend half the time with the animals. They're fascinated by them. Think of all the things in nature that you haven't experienced yet that are there to explore.

One of the most powerful experiences people have at my ranch is participating in a Native American sweat lodge ceremony. People love it. People with all types of religious beliefs benefit from the experience. There is no philosophy taught, merely experiences shared. People have a chance to see another belief system and are just blown away by it. It changes their perception of life. That will happen when you allow yourself the chance to get close to nature.

Where do you belong?

You need to look within for spiritual guidance to get an answer to this question. The conscious mind alone won't be able to help you. Ask yourself where, of all places, do you belong? Don't try to think through the answer—feel it instead.

Once you know where you belong, focus on being there. Affirm your answer by saying, here's where I feel I belong. Then it becomes a real possibility. Remember, with possibility there is action. With passion you create the action. With desire you create the passion and are able to get there.

The movie *Field of Dreams,* a metaphorical film about a midwestern corn farmer about to lose his farm, is a good example of this. The farmer keeps hearing a voice that says, "Build it and they will come." He follows his intuition and builds a little baseball field, and long-since-deceased players come back and play the game. His passion leads him to take action, and he makes an impossible dream happen. It's like reliving the fantasies of youth, where anything is possible.

You'll find that people who listen to their intuition and follow their dreams attract other people who support them in their efforts. Throughout the country you'll find people who did what no one thought was reasonable and succeeded because they had the support of someone else. It's that other person's way of reaching for the dream too.

How many times in your life have you heard a little voice inside you say, "Do the impossible, think the impossible, follow your dreams"? How often have you listened? When have you not?

What things do you fear?

I believe that you can live in a fulfilled and happy way and make anything real if you have the courage and confidence to try. That is what life is about. Once you define your new possibilities you have set the stage and are ready to start your journey.

You may not get there right away, but with planning you will get there. Don't give yourself an unrealistic timetable; it takes time to let go of things, unclutter your life, and heal from the elimination of the negative things you were attached to.

In the process, you are going to face changes that you fear. So ask yourself, what fears may keep me from getting started on my journey? Take on one thing that you fear each day. Write it down where you can see it. Look at what you've written and resolve it by affirming, this is how I'm going to deal with this fear today. Take action and you will be able to put fears away once and for all.

What would you do differently if there were no punishments and no rewards?

How much of what you do in a day is based upon punishment and reward? Looking at life that way helps you to see what you do to please others instead of what you do for yourself. It may get you to start saying what you need to say instead of what someone else wants to hear. You have every right to let people know if what they've giving you is enough or not enough, or whether it's right or needs to be changed.

Identify what is essential to your well-being. Don't be afraid to express feelings of excitement. People often think that as they grow older they should dull their passions when that's not true at all. You should explore your passions with the innocence and honesty of a child, and make everything a wonderful journey.

Part of you might say, I'd like to have this but I'm not sure it's acceptable. You might think what you want is too immature, so you hide your feeling of desire. But how do you know? Based upon what? Are you allowing someone else to tell you what you should want and believe in? Only you know what you need.

Do you live by opinions or knowledge?

A recent issue of the *Medical Tribune* reports a range of opinions that doctors have regarding vitamin E. Some of these doctors say that vitamin E is worthless. Others say you should have just the Recommended Daily Allowance. Still others think you need more. But no one has presented the fact that the scientific literature is filled with hundreds of examples of how vitamin E, at levels higher than the RDA, has benefited people with all kinds of conditions, from intermittent claudication to coronary heart disease. Knowledge ought to supersede opinion, yet many people speak their opinions without investigating whether or not they are based on truth.

Here's another example. People commonly accept as true the opinion that as you age you lose your libido. This is not necessarily so; there is no age at which your sex life necessarily diminishes. Society doesn't like to think of older people having a sex life, though, so it perpetuates this opinion. You see images of older people in movies as little old men and ladies in rocking chairs, or in advertisements as people troubled with hemorrhoids, or in a bathroom holding up their adult diapers. These images lead to your forming a one-sided opinion about older people that is not based on truth.

Think of all the beliefs you have that are based on opinion and not knowledge. For instance, you may believe that blacks are not as smart as whites, that women are not as emotionally stable as men, that going to an Ivy League school makes you smarter than others, that rich people are more successful than others at living. You may start equating money with happiness based on your opinion.

On the other hand, what have you done recently to gain real knowledge? When you gain knowledge, you gain power. And power gives you the confidence and courage to move on.

What excuses, emotions, or feelings do you use as distractions?

Do you distract yourself by getting angry, blaming, or becoming confused about what you want or need? These distracting feelings come from not trusting your inner guidance.

You need to trust your inner feelings about what you really want in all areas of life. Ask yourself, what kind of life do I want? Your age and other so-called limitations are immaterial. The only thing that matters is knowing what you want from your life. Once you know that, you can get anything.

The false starts come from not trusting your inner voice. You continue doing things you believe you should be doing but they don't feel right inside. This comes from following someone else's suggestions instead of your own.

This is not a child's game of choice played with a blindfold on. You can look around at what you may want. You can make your choice and then create a life around it. Otherwise, you're living a life limited by your circumstances, a life of adapting—adapting to your environment, to your job, to your social responsibilities, to your family—in short, to everyone else's needs. Constantly adapting distracts you from your own vision of life. Then your life doesn't work and it doesn't get any better tomorrow, next year, or ever.

So you've got to decide what you really want. You alone know what that is and you alone can choose to build a life around it. If you envision a certain type of house, for example, you will find a location and proceed to build your house. Otherwise, you might accept somebody else's dream and end up living in a well-manicured little suburban prison instead of the house in the country you envision for yourself.

You need to create a life based upon your own vision. Forget the excuses such as, nobody ever told me I could; I'm not smart enough; I don't have the resources. If other people can follow their dreams, so can you.

If Rupert Ravens, the man whose story I described earlier in this chapter, can create a food co-op, a health support group, a holistic health center, and begin a new book project—all in four weeks, with no education in that area and no money— think of what you can do. All you need is the desire and the willingness to follow your dreams. And of course you've got to get rid of what doesn't work and focus on what does.

Many people live busy lives but the busyness is nothing more than a series of distractions. They're not in touch with what they need to be doing for themselves. Rather, they're engaged in things that don't matter much and won't amount to anything.

Can you imagine your ideal job?

Imagine creating the type of job in which everything you put into your work matters, where what you do meets your real needs and fits your images and ideals. If it doesn't exist, create it, like in *Field of Dreams*. Build it and it will come true. Once you create the ideal job, people will pay attention to what you are doing. We're a service-oriented society. If you create the right service, people will want to support you.

Think of the people who have become successful just by doing the unusual. I talked with the owner of Celestial Seasonings, the tea company. He started his company in Boulder, Colorado, by going out with his knapsack and picking herbs from the sides of hills with a bunch of friends. He never let go of his ideal and now has a large, successful company.

Look at Ben & Jerry with their ethical ice cream company. They've created a good quality product that comes from a company that is socially conscious. They cared enough to create an organization based upon high standards.

People tried to discourage them from starting a company by telling them they were going to fail. But they listened to their inner direction instead and succeeded despite the naysayers because they believed in their dream and had the passion to follow it through.

There are many people who will support you in your dreams if you have the courage to honor and embrace them.

Eliminating Self-Defeating Habits

THERE ARE SEVERAL WAYS TO GO ABOUT OVERCOMING SELF-DEFEATING habits. One is to take an honest look at the part of your nature you generally try to hide, even from yourself, so that sometimes you are unaware of what you say and do and the consequences of your actions. Recently, for example, there was a rally in New York City against the Food and Drug Administration. It had a pretty good turnout—I'm guessing there were between 500 and 700 people present. Some people told me they had never protested at a demonstration before, and I complimented them for being there in order to encourage their efforts.

Then I started thinking about all the people who weren't there. At least 600,000 people listen to my radio show and knew about the rally's significance, and yet they weren't there. They never protest anything in their lives because they choose not to create discomfort.

I know the owner of a health food emporium who chose not to protest. I said to him, "Surely you know that your freedoms are being impinged upon. Since you sell vitamins, why couldn't you take the time to show your support?" He answered, "I was with you...." I immediately jumped in, "No, don't tell me you were with me in spirit. Either you participate in something or you don't." Although this man's livelihood is threatened if a law passes that bans vitamins, he chose to risk losing that rather than risk causing discomfort.

This seems analogous to the way many people live. They deceive themselves and try to fool others. They like to believe they are doing something when in actuality they're not. They like to believe they are really committed to changing what is wrong when in actuality they never get around to doing anything about it. They keep practicing their bad habits even as they complain and whine about their problems.

Men and women usually perpetuate bad habits differently. Women will generally talk openly and passionately about what is not working with their lives. They'll vent their feelings and discuss their problems, but not do anything to resolve them. In our society, women are encouraged to empathize with other women, which, up to a certain point, is a good thing. After that point, though, the conversation becomes pointless and frustrating.

Men, on the other hand, rarely complain about what is not working in their lives. They tend to intellectualize their problems away to keep from showing they are vulnerable. Men generally express few emotions. They show some joy and anger or rage, but are otherwise silent about their feelings, even among other men.

Let's begin with the idea that if you're going to make real changes happen you need to face your problems and do something about them, not simply vent them or pretend they're nonexistent. Start by looking at what you care about.

What do you care about?

Look at some issues that are important to you that you do nothing about. Our society professes concern for the environment, for example. Corporations now say they are environmentally conscious, although few really are. Most corporations' actions speak otherwise. For example, many of them dump more pesticides into the ocean than ever before.

The environmental movement in this country is very small. Maybe a thousand people in the entire nation work full-time to support an environmental cause such as Greenpeace, Friends of the Earth, or the Audubon Society. Only a thousand people remain between total abuse of our environment and our health.

Since the environment affects us all, why aren't we more committed as a nation to healing it? Why isn't it more of a priority? Why does an entire infrastructure have to disintegrate to the point at which it no longer functions before someone pays attention to it?

Again, there's an analogy on the personal level. The environmental situation can be compared to waking up one morning, looking in the mirror, and exclaiming, "My God, how did I get this way?" Nothing happens overnight. You don't get fat overnight. A marriage doesn't disintegrate in a day. You don't become alcoholic instantaneously. Things fall apart gradually as a result of neglect or abuse. If you wait too long, you no longer have a problem—you have a major, grade-A crisis.

Why not change what doesn't work? Why not be open and honest with yourself and decide what you really want from your work, your relationships, and your family? Why not simply change your priorities, since there is only so much time, energy, and emotion you can put into anything in one given day?

That may sound reasonable but most people focus on the obstacles, such as how their changing will affect others. People also tend to complacently accept their situations. I grew up in an town where the men never complained about anything, except maybe the outcome of the local high school football game. Everything else they accepted as a given. They were supposed to work in polluted factories, even if that meant inevitably contracting emphysema or lung cancer. To complain was unacceptable; it would be perceived as weak, unmasculine behavior.

These anti-change messages start early in life, when you're commanded to do as you've been told. You're a helpless, vul-

nerable little child. All you can do is feel; you can't yet intellectualize. You quickly learn, that if you disobey, you will be
punished, and if you obey you will be rewarded, even if the
reward only means not being punished. As a result you learn
to contain the real essence of your being. What should be
expressed isn't.

As an adult you continue to play by the rules to feel in-
cluded. If you're the only person at work really working, you
may be confronted with chidings such as "What are you doing? Slow down. Do you want to make us look bad?" Since
you don't want to rock the boat and make enemies, you start
to slow down. Fear of exclusion can be a powerful force.

What do you care about that you have neglected to care
for? What would you like to see change? What action can you
take to effect change?

Do you have outside support?

Your fantasies can make you different. They give you the impetus to explore your dreams. They make you feel you can be
anybody. You believe you contain the power to change anything.

Then one day you wake up and are told that you can't do
anything. You have to stay in your place. Families are frequently the first people to give you that message. Instead of
giving support, they tell you you're wrong for feeling different. If you start living up to your potential you become a
reflection of what they might have been had they tried. You
remind them that they didn't have courage. You're threatening them by saying, in effect, that they've lived an unactualized life. They never became who they really could have been,
but instead chose to be who their father, mother, and others
told them they should be. They were obedient, and now they
no longer feel the pain because they've anesthetized themselves to it. They've lost touch with anything vital and essential to their own natures and they've forgotten their real
needs.

You, on the other hand, want to be who you really are so you don't feel conflicted and contradicted. You don't want to walk around in a thousand bits and pieces; you want to feel whole.

Search out people with goals similar to yours. Associate with people whose standards are better than yours or more specific and stronger so that you have to raise yours. They'll make you stretch and reach new heights. When I train, I want to train with people who are better and faster than I am. That pushes me. When I have a conversation, I want to talk to someone who is smarter than I am and who has something to add.

The whole issue is one of self-actualization. Shouldn't you count? Shouldn't your time and energy be prioritized around what is important to you? When it isn't, two years, five years, twenty years fly by and you haven't spent time on you. Everything else has gotten your attention and emotions but you. As a result, you feel angry and resentful. Then you start to burn up and implode. To call that scenario unhealthy is an understatement.

Write about a dream that you want to actualize. Have you shared that dream with anyone? Have those people given you negative feedback, or support? What is the result of that interaction? Dreams are fragile; be careful about whom you enlist for support.

Why are you attracted to someone?

One reason you're drawn to another person is that you're seeing a reflection of what you ideally see in yourself. The other person becomes the surrogate you. You fantasize about what the other person will fulfill for you, and the idea of that fulfillment keeps the attraction alive.

You can be attracted to someone for any number of reasons. Sometimes they're the wrong reasons; sometimes the right ones. It's okay to be attracted to someone because he or she is good looking. There's nothing wrong with that. But of course you also have to care about what lies beyond the looks. You have to evaluate the nature of the person to see whether she or he has a warm heart, if he or she is caring and accepting. It's okay to need things from people if those things help you to be a more healthy, happy person, but it's destructive to need things that result in a disempowering relationship. Be clear about what you need.

One of the biggest problems that can come up in a relationship is dishonesty.

Honesty and trust are basic to a healthy relationship. It doesn't matter if your partner is sexy and fun to be with if you know the person is going to betray you. I know men who will stay with women who betray them because all they're concerned about is having good sex. That's all some men think about. I know women who choose to be with attractive, sexy men, without asking themselves what other qualities an ideal mate would have.

You may stay in a relationship to have someone take care of you. The price you pay is becoming dependent rather than self-reliant. You become limited because you've never attempted to expand your horizons to see what you are capable of becoming. Instead, you only continue to perpetuate basic skills. Your position in your family becomes all-important.

What happens, though, when the children grow up? Many women go through a crisis when their children leave home. It's because they have no one to be dependent *for*. If the purpose of your relationship was to have a family and you haven't made any life for yourself, one day the family is gone and you're forty or older, feeling empty, alone, and abandoned. Some mothers continue to attach themselves to their adult children, trying to play a role in their lives that goes beyond that of a parent. They meddle and try to make decisions for their children because they haven't developed a life of their own.

Do you fear intimacy?

Most men in our society have a terrible time expressing intimacy because of the intensity of relating that accompanies it. They want autonomy and intimacy at the same time. They want the benefits of attachment and relating and having their needs met, but they also want to be able to step aside and say, "I don't feel like being intimate now."

Women, generally speaking, are conditioned to enjoy intimacy and openness within a relationship. They have no problem sharing their feelings. These differences between women and men in our culture may cause difficulties within a relationship. One person sees intimacy as a positive thing; the other uses intimacy as a way of establishing that he's needed, but then takes a step back from the relationship. You can see the possibility for problems when you have two styles of relating that don't mesh.

Being sexual is not the same as being intimate. Intimacy leaves you open and vulnerable. It is more difficult than being sexual because it allows others to see your imperfections. Men generally are afraid their vulnerability will be used against them. Women don't want to be too open as a rule because they fear rejection. If you're telling people what you really think and feel about things essential to you, and others reject your thoughts as unacceptable, it's as if they're rejecting you.

Your beliefs about yourself dictate how freely you confide in someone. I was out running with a bunch of guys. One of them, an artist, said some things out of the blue that two of the other guys were shocked at hearing. Later, one of the guys said, "I can't believe he told us those things." I said, "Why not? He's a very open person. Also, his belief system is autonomous. You and I will not affect the way he thinks. He's not afraid of us, nor is he in competition with us. Therefore he's willing to be open and to share his innermost feelings."

I added, "Wouldn't it be nice if you could tell your innermost secrets without fear, knowing that there was no way that you would be rejected because of them?" He replied, "Man, I have too many things I can't tell people. If I did, they would think I was some kind of kook." Yes, the likelihood is that you will be rejected and scorned for many of your innermost beliefs. As a result, most people show one side of themselves and hide another.

Some time ago, I did a special about who goes to prostitutes. I interviewed about fifteen street prostitutes, some call girls, and some escorts. The most interesting interview was with an escort who told me that her primary clients don't have sex with her, at least after the first time. The first time they think it's a prerequisite. Once they feel confident and comfortable with her, they just talk.

I asked her what they talk about and she said, "Simple things. They talk to me about things they're afraid to talk to their wives or buddies about." I asked her who these man are and she told me they come from all walks of life. A lot of them, however, are in management and government positions. They're afraid to talk openly with people around them because they have an image to maintain. What they tell her shows that these men live with fear and uncertainty. They're afraid to project their vulnerabilities. Even their families have this idea that these men are good providers who are strong, forceful, and dynamic, when that's not who they are at all. She said, "I know some men who the world perceives as dynamic and outgoing, but to me they're terrified little boys. They come to me because I'm the only person who is not going to use that against them." She added, "It's interesting how much better they feel after talking to me. It's as though I'm their therapist. I feel bad for them." What a society we have when people are terrified of telling anyone about their real feelings for fear that they will be used against them!

Are you able to express intimacy? Is it easy or difficult for you? In whom do you confide?

Where do you yearn to belong?

If you are like most people, you want to belong to something. Belonging verifies who you are and makes you feel connected. You may be a loner, but if you join a club and go to meetings, you're in a sense no longer alone. Suddenly you count because you're a part of something, even if you're one member in a million.

I do not mean to imply for a second that you shouldn't belong to a club or organization. Joining one is a completely legitimate thing to do. I do, though, want to bring up the question of your maintaining the autonomy to make decisions for yourself while being a member. Some organizations allow you that and some don't.

The danger is that, in order to stay in an organization, you may have to give up your critical feelings about what doesn't work. Usually, you can't stay in an organization and at the same time oppose it. There's an understanding that if you're going to join anything you'd better accept that which you are joining almost unconditionally. So, for instance, if you are supporting a presidential candidate, you have to accept that person completely, even his or her obvious limitations. You must overlook these because you have committed yourself to a cause.

If you look at what a person belongs to, frequently you can get a good handle on who the person is. Some people, for instance, belong to non-mainstream movements like vegetarian societies, or the yoga movement. They will adapt much of their lifestyles to embracing the principles of their particular cause. All of these movements have something important to contribute.

This doesn't mean, however, that the people running them are always balanced or necessarily doing the right thing. Often they're concerned only with maintaining power and control. This frustrates people and results in their leaving organizations that, ideally, they'd like to be committed to. I've met people who have gotten out of the animal rights movement because of some of the acts committed by people within the organization, such as throwing dye on people wearing animal furs. Such assaults go beyond expressing one's philosophy to transgress a boundary, and, as a result, a lot of people won't join the animal rights movement who otherwise might have.

Groups may benefit you to a point, but be careful not to lose your identity. Joining an organization for a period of time may give you valuable information and link you to others with similar beliefs but don't automatically take on the group's values. Question what you are told, and accept only what feels right to you. The important thing to remember is that you must not feel compelled to accept what doesn't work for you. Take what works, use it, and let go of what doesn't work.

Look at where you yearn to belong. When you feel very alone and you're unable to express your ideas, you will generally join an organization that helps you feel more powerful through mutual support. The more helpless you feel, the greater the energy you need from the organization.

The same is true in a relationship. If you feel weak and unactualized, you're going to look for qualities in another person that compensate for deficiencies. You want someone to say, for example, "Don't worry. I'm successful. I have the intellect to figure things out." That person will try to be responsible for you and many people find comfort in that. But that doesn't guarantee that that person is going to take away your problems or pain.

Again, we should always be asking questions. What do we care about? What are we bringing to that area of life? Are we rejecting what we should care about? In joining something, or in a relationship, are we allowed to be autonomous or not? To what degree do we want to be autonomous? To what degree do we want to be empowered?

Once we answer these questions we can begin to make changes and be attached to the right things openly and completely without fear of intimacy. When we have an open and intimate relationship we can thrive. That's where happiness and balance occur.

Stop Blaming, Start Growing

FREQUENTLY WE TRY TO ACHIEVE GOALS THAT OTHER PEOPLE SET FOR us. We take courses in college we don't want to take but think we should. We work in jobs we really don't like but think we should keep because other people tell us we're lucky to have a job. I interviewed coal miners in England and found that not one out of 200 was happy with life. In fact, they thought that my question about happiness was a stupid question. They had no concept of creating a happy, fulfilling life, and thought that the way past generations had lived was the way they should live. It was all they knew, and they saw no other options. They would even justify their way of life. "I work myself to the bone for what I have." "I don't have very much as it is." "If I tried anything else I wouldn't have anything." "How would I support my family?" Not one person I interviewed expressed a passion for living. Their mood was somber. Life was terrible.

It's the same way in America to a large degree. People learn not to have desires because the moment they express them someone makes discouraging remarks. When you envision changes, you are told, "What are you thinking about that for? How are you going to pay the rent?" You start thinking they're right, that it is indeed foolish of you to have a desire. It's easy to see how desire gets lost.

People start to give up and live in an escapist fantasy world, which is why so many people mail in sweepstakes entries and invest in the lottery. People have stopped believing in their own creative initiative. They want something more but don't know how to go about getting it.

Why not choose to make your life different if that's what it takes to make it work? Who says it has to be difficult? I believe the opposite is true. It's really easy to make your life work. I find it's easy to be healthy. Just eat what is natural and real and leave the rest alone. It's also easy to be with people by confronting situations as they arise instead of holding them in. On the other hand, I find it difficult to hold on to something that doesn't work and then try to justify it. It's also difficult to think negative thoughts, project negative deeds, do destructive things and then try to rationalize them. These activities don't make any sense to me, so they're difficult for me to engage in.

Dealing with life honestly and openly becomes progressively easier. You get into a pattern of making the right decisions each day. You need to tune into the little voice inside of you that is connected with the subconscious mind. People are used to hearing the conscious mind all the time. That's the mind that makes almost all their decisions. The conscious mind is rational. It tries to project a public image. But the subconscious mind is always honest. It has not been changed by conditioning. It is eternal.

In order to master life you've got to be honest about what you do that keeps your life from working. Then you can focus on what will make it work. Again, it starts with desire. At the top of your list, note what you've always desired but not paid attention to because you felt guilt from the conscious mind telling you all the reasons you couldn't follow through with your desire. Desire is not the pathology you've been led to believe it is.

First of all, stop the idea that you have to justify your life. If you're like many people, about half your time is spent justifying yourself to other people in the work you do, in the emotions you have, in the relationships you have. This continual justification is a big distraction that causes you to lose focus on what you're doing. And focus is important. The most productive people are the ones who can maintain their focus on whatever work they're doing at the moment, the way a professional ball player keeps focused on the ball.

Start by honoring you: It's your life. You're the only one who is going to live it. No one else has the right to tell you who you are, what you are, and how you're going to live. So give yourself room to breathe by letting others know how they're affecting you. Be up front with people. Say, for instance, "Mom, don't call me every day to see if I'm getting married or not. It's my life, not yours. I'm the one who's going to get married if and when I want to." All it takes is the courage to say to someone, "Sorry, but if you didn't call to support me and share something positive, please don't call. I'm not angry; I have started to take control of my life and I need positive reinforcement so that I can grow."

Sure the status quo of your relationship is going to be threatened when you do this. But threatening the status quo is sometimes part of the challenge of mastering life.

No matter what happens each day, I never lose my focus on what the day is, what it can mean, what I want the day to mean. I have a desire to make that day work. Do you think I'd be doing my radio shows or this book, or all the other things I do if it weren't for the fact that part of what I have to do in life is offer service to society? I don't feel bad if people are mad at me for trying to help them, because I never lose my focus. I don't get angry either because anger would only be a distraction from that focus.

Be confident of your ability to make right decisions. You have to go inside to do that. Learn not to be afraid of what other people will say when you make the decisions that are right for you.

How many times have you refrained from doing something because you were afraid the other people in your life would not approve? You were more concerned about their approval than you were about making a right decision. How many times in your life have you made the wrong decision because it was more important to have someone accept you than it was for you to accept the right thing for yourself? It happens all the time because being accepted is very important to people.

Honoring your true self seems to be a secondary consideration until something is lost—until you end up overweight, for instance, or until you end up socially stressed and in a crisis. Then you realize that you've been making wrong decisions, and that it's time to start making right ones for a change. For this, you need support.

Where does your support come from?

As you grow and change you're going to need support in many areas. Consider where you can get support for each of these aspects of your life.

Emotional

Make a list of the people and groups who give you emotional support. Are you getting enough, or is emotional support lacking? If you need emotional support for the changes you want to make, there is no shortage of places that offer it. There are twelve-step programs, for example, and all kinds of other groups that support change. For every homemaker who wants to get out of the home, there are women's advocacy groups that are out there to help her. There are men's advocacy groups helping them to understand what it is to be a real man and not just a superficial stereotypical model of one. It's easy enough to locate these groups: simply look in the Yellow Pages under self-help or support groups. A recent scanning found more than forty different groups.

Remember, change is a long-term process and you've got to have emotional support you can count on. If you don't have it, look for it. It's not going to come to you. You're going to have to be assertive and find the people who will support you without criticizing, condemning, or trying to manipulate you.

Financial

Getting financial support from people means more than getting money from them. Frequently, it takes the form of advice that will help you improve the quality of your life. Someone might listen to me lecture and respond by saying, "It all sounds nice, Gary, but I'm living on $32,000 a year. Sure, I'd really like to change; I do feel stagnant. I've lived in the same place for so long and I'd like to be someplace else. I've got some things I'd like to do. But I can't afford any of them."

My response would be, "You're right and you're wrong. You're right in that you can't afford change if you're not looking for options. You're wrong because people without much money also try to change their lifestyles and many succeed. I can show you people who have wonderful lifestyles. They're deprived of nothing they feel they need and they're living lives radically different from those they used to live. They've learned to change and do without many of the unnecessary trappings of life."

Let me tell you about a technique I use each year. You may or may not find this useful. I never start a new project before stopping an old one. I even give up things that are profitable. I stop them and just let them go. People think this is the dumbest thing in the world. "My God," they say, "you took so much time and energy and commitment to create something and now that it's succeeding you're giving it up? Why?"

I feel that if I start doing more things than what I can reasonably take on, then I don't have a balanced life. And I believe that having a balanced life is so important that I'm willing to give things up to support the balance. In doing so, I have more time for myself, and I have the opportunity to do something different.

As I start a new project I ask myself, do I want this to be a one-year, two-year, three-year, four-year, or five-year project? I don't do anything longer than five years. I can't see doing anything longer than that.

Think about what would be different in your life if you

were told you had five years to live. Would you start doing things differently? Frequently what you would start doing is what you really want to do. Find ways of doing it now.

Part of the art of living and mastering life is the art of letting go. The more you let go, the more you have room and freedom for better things. Every year I try to give away as much as I can. This is a big challenge when you come from a background where you never had anything. I come from a very poor background. I've been working since the age of eight, and nothing has been given to me at any point in life, so to be able to give things away is a challenge. Being strict about getting rid of things makes you realize what you can live without. If you don't learn to let go of things then you just have clutter.

A friend of mine recently went through a major crisis over his uncertainty about his career of twenty-two years. Finally, in one absolutely nerve-wracking weekend, he let go of his career and went through withdrawal, crisis, and a lot of depression. Two days later, he was offered an opportunity to do something that was wonderful for him even though it was only a six-month project. I advised him not to look for projects that were going to take him through the rest of his life, but for projects that act as transition points, that will take him to a new level.

Right now he's living in Arizona on a dude ranch. Here's what's amazing. We were watching the film *City Slickers,* and all through the film he kept saying, "I'd love to do that." And then the day came when someone gave him the opportunity to do it. The first words out of his mouth were all negative: "I don't have the money and I've never ridden a horse. . . ." I said to him, "Hold on. Give me ten reasons why you would like to do it and how you could. If you had stopped with the negatives you wouldn't have done it, but you went ahead and showed that you can do it." That's what I'm talking about— look for the reasons why.

Intellectual

What education do you need in order to do what you want to do? One nice thing about the United States is that we have more classes, workshops, and adult education than any other country in the world. We are a nation filled with rejuvenation and growth. Look at the Learning Annex here in New York City. Look at all the classes and workshops. Look at the 92nd Street Y and all their lectures and workshops. You can get any skills you need. And you can barter for services if you don't have the money, through a practice called creative scholarship exchanges. There's always something you have that will help someone else, and they in turn will help you. Virtually every organization, individual, or group has a need for parttime assistance—helping with mailing, answering mail, filing, and the like. Generally, if you approach the office manager and explain that because of a temporary shortage of funds you're not able to pay but would be able to work parttime in exchange for the classes, they can probably accommodate you. After all, the lecture is their "product," and having one more person in a class does not take away any of their income. Speaking for myself, I have never given a lecture or workshop or retreat where several people didn't approach me to say that they wanted to attend but couldn't afford it. I never refused a soul and am sure others are of like mind.

List your special attributes and skills

Often you're not even aware of how special you are. You're not cognizant of your skills and attributes. Write them down. Many of your attributes may be the result of having gotten through crises, or the crises may have shown you that you had them all along. Think of all the crises in your life that you've weathered. In all likelihood you've already weathered the very things you've feared the most. You've probably already gone through separations, deaths, firings—a lot of things that are traumatizing and high up on the stress scale. You've survived and are stronger for your experiences. If you think along these lines, nothing should create fear now.

We've all experienced humiliations. We've all gone through these processes and we've survived. That's what's nice about an AA or an OA meeting. You get people to stand up and say what they've done and how they have survived. They're acknowledging that they have a life beyond their crippling experiences.

What have you survived? How are you stronger from the experience? What special attributes did you learn you have as a result of what you've been through?

Do you sabotage your own efforts?

Watch to see whether you sabotage your own efforts. The moment you start feeling a little depressed or unfocused, do you undermine your efforts so that you need to start all over? An example of this would be going on an eating binge when you've been trying to reform your diet.

Watch the process of self-sabotage. List ways you engage in it. If you have a really close friend, or if you're part of a support group, let someone know what you do to sabotage yourself. Ask the person for help when you start hurting yourself. A little support goes a long way. Hopefully in time you'll be your own best support system.

Do your inner beliefs and outer realities complement each other?

Believing in one thing and doing another generates conflict. It creates a psychic spasm. Check to see whether you live according to your own beliefs or according to other people's. How many times have you adopted behaviors inconsistent with your inner feelings because you felt you should be loyal to people? You need not honor them out of some bizarre loyalty. Think of how many people on the inside knew that our country shouldn't have been involved in Operation Desert Storm. They went along because everyone else was wrapping themselves up in loyalty to the flag and being patriotic. They were living a double standard and causing conflict within themselves.

Don't be afraid to commit yourself to whatever you feel in your heart, even if you feel that you're in the minority. When you acknowledge what's in your heart, you are getting in touch with spiritual truth. If spiritual truth is on your side, you're a majority of one.

Are you able to forgive?

What unresolved conflicts are you still holding onto? Unresolved conflicts keep you from getting on with your life because you give them all your attention.

There's a time when you've got to give them up. You have to stop feeling sorry for yourself and angry because someone betrayed and used you, or because you didn't do more with your life. Start perceiving unfortunate things that have happened to you as nothing more than learning experiences, and let them go. Now you're right on track.

There are a million ways to forgive. Every religion and every belief has a way of forgiving. But in order for forgiveness to happen, you have to first realize that you no longer need to invest in the pain that came from the original indiscretion or abuse. You have to make your life more important than your pain. The original pain is gone. All you're living with now is the memory of that pain. That's not very smart, is it? And it's not being kind to yourself either. It was bad enough that you were abused, disregarded, or hurt as a human being. Now you're compounding the damage by living with something long after the experience. You're revolving your life around painful memories. That keeps you from expressing your true self and functioning as a whole, dynamic, integrated human being.

Give it up. You don't need a lifetime to do it. You don't need thirty-five workshops with all the currently popular leaders out there telling you all about your mother and father and what they did to you. You know that already. Just say to yourself, "My life's more important than the memory of that pain."

You're more than just your experiences. You're a living entity with a capacity to create, feel, and grow. Yes, you have experiences that you can draw feelings and emotions from, but you shouldn't become merely the feelings and emotions of your experience. I know a woman who was raped by a black man on the subway when she was sixteen. Today, she hates all blacks. He didn't rape her because he was black; he could have been any color, but in her heart she formed a hatred against all black people. Her whole reality has become distorted based on her perception of what caused her pain.

Experiences can give you an understanding of life, and you can learn just as much from negative experiences as from positive ones. That doesn't mean that if you have a bad experience you yourself have to become negative. You don't have to start feeling bad about yourself just because someone says something to you that's uncomplimentary. That would allow the person to manipulate you, which doesn't make a whole lot of sense. Your self-esteem goes down when you allow an experience to be more essential to you than your own inner dynamics. All that an experience should do is give you a greater understanding of life.

Once I was invited to participate at a feminist meeting, but I never got the chance to talk. If I had gotten a chance to, the audience would have heard about the spiritual feminist perspective as viewed through a male perspective. But the people at that meeting were not into hearing anything of a spiritual feminist nature. In fact, the woman who headed the meeting had a very hateful attitude toward men. I did not overreact to the situation. I felt the woman supported a particularly radical political and sexist position, not a spiritually and humanistically feminist one. But she had a right to that.

I know that another workshop that I'm invited to will have a completely different perspective. What I'm saying is that you shouldn't jump to angry or defensive stances based on individual experiences. Allow them to be what they are—individual experiences.

Living defensively keeps you from mastering life. You need to be vulnerable. Otherwise you have all sorts of problems. You become fat, stressed out, angry, locked in the past, and full of excuses. You blame the world because your life isn't working.

Where in your life do you live defensively? You've got to deal with this, so look at your biases, notice your conditioned beliefs, and acknowledge them for what they are. Clean them out or you'll be carrying them around forever.

When you defend wrong beliefs you become defensive about it. When people want to defend the merits of their beliefs they'll pass a law. The state of Illinois passed a law this year, for example, that made pregnancy a condition that doctors exclusively must treat. The law passed despite a New Mexico health study done over an eleven-year period that shows midwives to be more effective at helping women give birth, at far less cost. Their death rates are lower and they have a five-percent cesarean section rate as opposed to the twenty-seven-percent rate that obstetricians have. The state of Illinois ignores the evidence and excludes midwives from participating in the birthing process with their new law. That is simply a wrong belief. And the fact that it is law institutionalizes it.

Once something becomes law people start to think it's beyond question. Of course, the law can be challenged and amended but that's quite difficult because, unfortunately, people tend to be more focused on obeying the law than on examining its merits, or asking whether it is just. The average person won't challenge the law. In fact, most people won't challenge anything that's wrong. They won't challenge the quality of their food, air, soil, or anything else. Instead, they've come to accept things as they are because they haven't challenged their own lives. If you're not challenging your own life and what doesn't work within it, you'll certainly never challenge what is outside of your own life.

How do you react to negative experiences? What can you learn from them? List the feelings you have that are not completely reasonable and rational. What experiences are you reacting to?

Whom do you blame for your problems and feelings?

If you're going to master life and live happily, you've got to stop blaming. People who want to master life don't blame; they take control of their lives. Did you ever notice that the people out there who are trying and learning make more mistakes than anybody else, yet they never blame anybody for them? They just get back up and try again. I counseled a woman last year who blamed everything on everybody and everything. She projected her anger on others instead of taking responsibility for making her life work. She spent all her time blaming and had no time left for action. That person was no better when she stopped counseling than when she started.

Blamers are people who, when they try and fail, seem to fall in cement. They get stuck in their failure. All they look at is the pain and anger of their failure, and who they can blame for it. If you get caught up in blaming, you stop growing. Show me someone who blames and I'll show you someone who hasn't grown since the day they began to blame. Their life stops; it's like they're dead. People blame because they're looking for an escape. Blaming is just a way of keeping their minds from looking for constructive solutions.

When you make a commitment to do something new, accept that you're going to make mistakes. It's alright to fail. That's a part of life. It's how you'll grow and learn. Once you stop blaming, you'll have room to grow. You'll become more interested in what you're doing than in the consequences of not doing it right. Something good happens when you take on that attitude.

When you develop the right attitude you're not going to be afraid to take some major risks. The people I know whose lives have succeeded have taken lots of risks. They've had many failures, but a lot of rewards too. In fact, I've never met anyone who succeeds at life who doesn't take risks. At some point you have to realize that without risks there is no reward. What risks are you willing to take? No risks? No reward. Small risks? Small reward. Take a big risk, get a big reward.

What risks are you willing to take to get where you want to go? Does fear of failure stop you? Do you blame others when things don't work out, or do you see it as part of the learning process?

Are your limitations real?

Is your whole life bounded by limitations? How real are they? Who put them there? How long have these limitations been there? What have you done to adapt to them?

People tell me what they can't do. They never tell me what they can do. The moment they say, "I don't think . . ." I stop them and say, "Then why are you here? If you talk that way you'll never get anywhere."

I work with people who say can do, will do, here I am, let's do it. It's no big deal. It's simple. The people who want to do, do it. The people who don't, make excuses.

Start to listen to how people talk. Listen to the excuses.

Limitations should not be set before you try something. Otherwise your conditioned responses, which come largely from the experiences and the input of other people, will dictate what you're willing to try. This places artificial limitations in front of you. Think of how many senior citizens in our society never set foot inside a health club because of a social image they adhere to. They don't believe they ought to mix with the younger culture. Working out isn't something they should be doing. They think that instead of keeping fit they should be staying at home rocking on their porches and taking medicines. Because of an artificial limitation they've placed on themselves, they're missing out on something that could be of enormous benefit.

What would you like to do but feel you can't? What limitations do you perceive? Look for role models to follow if that's what it takes to get started. Look at where you've been successful in your own life despite your conditioning to the contrary. What have you done that you were not expected to do?

What price do you pay for success?

We've been talking largely about failure. Now let's consider success. You are probably successful in some area of your life, perhaps several. What price do you pay for your success? Are you stressed out, for example? How does that stress affect you? Does the stress equal the benefits? Is it balanced by the success?

It's rare to find a person we call successful in our society's conventional sense that doesn't end up paying a big price for that success. I've counseled many successful people. This past summer I worked with an internationally known artist who was enormously stressed. He was afraid to turn jobs down even though he was overworked. He couldn't say no to all the commissions. I asked him why he didn't just take a year off. After all, he had plenty of money. He said he was terrified of taking a step backward. Someone else might come in and take his place. This man is a prisoner of his own success. His drive to go on and on creates a pressure that will ultimately destroy the quality of what he has succeeded at.

Our society tends to praise successful people, often giving them more praise than they deserve. Two people will go into a boxing ring to beat each other up and get more praise and recognition than all of the Nobel Prize winners in history. In America, success gives you access. People suddenly pay attention to you, whether you deserve it or not.

Once successful, people become fearful of losing this attention and try to hold on to that success more tightly than ever, like the artist I counseled. They're afraid they might lose it all. If you don't fight, you get stripped of your crown. In broadcasting and television, with rare exceptions, the moment you go off the air, no matter how popular you are, it's almost impossible to get back on. The same is true for writers. Once you stop publishing, you're forgotten. As a result, most successful people don't know how to say no.

Seeking success to gain public approval will make you insecure and apprehensive. The public is fickle, and if you start to fail in any way it will withdraw its support of you. As much as we're enamoured with people climbing up the ladder of success we don't like to associate with someone on his way down. Once you're down nobody will help you get back up; we're very hard on people who are trying to make a comeback. So people end up constantly striving, terrified of losing status.

We make success almost impossible to sustain while staying happy and healthy. I think it's because our society doesn't encourage people to make mistakes and to learn from their failures. We don't allow people to show their flaws once they've attained a hero's status. For instance, we want to keep Pete Rose out of the Hall of Fame for betting on his own team, even though that has nothing to do with his status as a great athlete.

We need to keep balanced and realize that success is more than financial, more than public adulation. Success is how you grow on nonmaterial levels as well. Success can be internal. It can be learning to relate to people well, growing spiritually and emotionally. You can be successful in any area of life. Go forward because you want to learn and enjoy life. If you're only motivated by your fear then you're still a prisoner, you're not balanced, and you're not mastering anything.

What have you had it with?

An effective way to focus on changing your life is to write on a piece of paper the things you've had it with. In a prominent place, such as on your mirror or refrigerator, or on your desk at work, place a little sign that reads, "I've had it with _____."

That will focus your attention on what needs to be changed. In that moment when you say, "I've had it!" you are facing your life truthfully. You're being honest. You're saying, "I'm out of here. I'm changing this." You've reached your limit. It's the last straw. You've tolerated too much abuse, indifference, or imbalance, and you've had enough.

Do this each day. Ask, what have I had it with? What am I going to change? This exercise eliminates a big buffer zone for excuses and adaptations. Remember, you're extremely adaptable. You keep adapting to what doesn't work. If something doesn't work, you twist, you turn, you contort yourself emotionally because you've adapted to so many different things that aren't you. Straighten up and say, "I've had it. I'm not wearing anything that I don't like. I'm not saying anything I don't believe. I'm not doing anything that doesn't honor me. I'm not relating to people who don't respect who I am."

Making an "I've had it" list each day will not only help you see what works and what doesn't work in your life, it will give you the courage and the impetus to actually make change happen. A friend of mine had been overweight and a hypochondriac for over twenty years. One day I asked him, "Have you had it?" and he said he had. He made a list of the things he had had it with and one of the things on his list was compulsive overeating. He ate a lot of junk foods. I said, "Now that you've made a list, do you want to change?", and he said yes.

We took the food from the cupboards and threw away everything that wasn't good. We threw away *everything*. His heart was palpitating as I chanted, "Junk, junk, junk." Not only did we throw food away, we stomped up on it. I even put food on top of the toilet as a symbolic gesture. I said, "This is crap. It belongs down the toilet, not in your body." When we finished I said, "Now that you've got it all out, keep it out."

This was a painful process for my friend, who was actually sweating as he let all this go. It was traumatic for him, but at the end of the day he had a whole new kitchen full of healthful foods and cookbooks that we bought. He later hired a person to come in once a week to cook lots of good food and freeze it for him. He joined an overeater's support group and each day called someone to make sure he stayed on his plan. He took it day by day.

Today he is of normal weight, in perfect health, and wouldn't go back to his old ways for anything. It took him over two decades, but it started on the day he said, "I've had it."

Make a list of the things you've had it with. During the week, select one item you need to change. When you feel balanced in that area, deal with the next item on your list.

Creating a Healthy Goal

Do you stop yourself short of your goal? Perhaps you allow whatever feelings you wake up with to dictate your actions for the rest of the day. If you wake up feeling good, then everything seems possible. If you start the day feeling bad, you hold yourself back. You don't believe you can do what you set out to do, and make excuses to keep yourself from getting things done. In effect, you make something or someone out there responsible for how you feel inside. You wake up waiting for bits and pieces of light to hit you and make you feel good about who you are, instead of affirming that you are always in the light. The trouble is, once you take a step past the light you're back in the dark again. Now it's just another day, there's another person to deal with, another occurrence; that nice little ray of sunlight is no longer hitting you.

The danger in thoughts like these is that you start to believe that you can't motivate yourself. In the absence of self-sustained positive energy you become helpless and hapless. You start looking for excuses to justify your lack of initiative and, as a result, you never fulfill your personal goals.

Life becomes different when you realize that every step you take in life is illuminated with eternal love and joy. This is something that preceded you and will be here long after you are gone. Knowing there is light and love within you wherever you go promotes a true sense of happiness.

This knowledge kindles the desire to take appropriate risks for the joy of it. Every action you take naturally sets off a chain of events. If something good happens and you receive a

162

reward, that's fine. But if it doesn't, that's alright too. What you do is not going to be predicated upon whether or not it makes you feel good. Instead, you will already feel good when you wake up, and you will sustain that good feeling no matter what happens.

Don't wait for someone or something out there to acknowledge that you're okay. Get out of your own way and make a life for yourself. Learn to use your mind positively and don't worry; worrying never accomplishes anything. Use the mind in a relaxed, natural way. That allows you to explore life for the curiosity, wonderment, joy, grace, innocence, and honesty of it. Dare to be different. Life is about taking appropriate risks. They're what make it worth living.

Let's explore some reasons why you may get in your own way and keep yourself from creating and achieving healthy goals.

What are you uncertain of?

Uncertainties can keep your life in a state of perpetual postponement. So it's important to look at what you're uncertain of and then deal with it. Look at the following areas of your life to determine how uncertainty holds you back.

Fantasies

Fantasies will impede you if you retreat into them instead of using them as a catalyst for constructive change. If you're working at a boring job, for example, you could fantasize about working someplace else but not follow up and make plans that can lead to change. You could stay there, spending most of the day engaged in escapist thoughts. But imagine what could happen if you were to put effort into making your fantasy into reality. Who's to say it couldn't happen?

The mind is powerful. It can take you to new heights, but it can also constrain you. The other day, for example, I worked with three people who have just committed themselves to racing nationally. They want to be as healthy and as fast as they can possibly be. These are not elite athletes; they're just normal people who dream of becoming athletes. I pushed them very hard. One person said, "I can't go a seven-minute mile. I've never gone faster than a nine-minute mile." Ten minutes later when I had the treadmill on, I didn't tell him what he was doing. I just encouraged him to go a little faster. He was working at a seven-minute mile pace and was keeping up with it.

After the first mile, I said, "Now I'm going to take you into the seven-minute range." He gasped, "I can't do it; it's too hard." He had already done it at that time but when I put it into his mind that he was going to have to do it, he pulled back.

He was completely surprised when I told him he already did it. That's the power the mind can have over the body—it's not always a positive power. The demon inside says, "Can't do it. Can't do it. Can't do it."

If you ever think you can't do something because you're not as talented or capable as someone else perhaps you don't know what you are capable of doing. The only thing standing between you and your higher self is you. Don't worry about what other people are doing. All you can do is the best *you* can do. Honor that, whatever it is. You may even learn that you are more capable and talented than you ever conceptualized. But nothing will ever happen until you allow yourself to actualize your creative fantasies.

Intuition

Intuitively, you know what feels right. The problem occurs when the conscious mind tries to rationalize your feelings away. Inside you know the honesty and integrity of the people you're dealing with. The internal self never lies. It gives you a signal to either stop or go.

Are you able to differentiate the signals your heart sends

from the signals of the mind? Notice how the mind steps in and creates chaos, pain, and confusion that blocks you. Let your intuition be your guide; don't be a prisoner of the rational mind.

Commitment

You may feel uncertain about what you want to commit yourself to. You may not know what to do with your life. Remember that commitment is not just a matter of enjoyment but integral to your growth as a human being. It allows you to connect with something greater than your own life, something spiritual. It gives your life meaning.

If you don't commit yourself to something higher than yourself, then you are committing yourself to your lower nature, concentrating on such things as indulgences and distractions. Distractions are acceptable as long as they're kept in perspective. But when money and other signs of outward success become your focus, then you don't really have a life. One day you wake up, look in the mirror, and think, "My God, look how old I've gotten, and what have I got to show for it? What have I committed myself to?" You've devoted yourself to wrong values and wrong decisions based upon insecurity, invulnerability, and being a prisoner of the rational mind. You have all the things you thought would make you happy and you don't have happiness.

The key is, can you be happy with none of the things that you worked so hard to get? If you can, then you're a truly happy person.

Think for a moment. What is the most important thing you've committed yourself to in the past year? Is it something as important as, or more important than, your own life?

Are your expectations realistic?

I was helping a racewalker train when he commented that he wanted to start running instead of racewalking. I asked him why and he responded that he didn't think he was a fast racewalker. I reassured him that I thought he was fast. We discussed the fact that if he ran he would probably run a 6.5-minute mile. Since people in his age group are doing between 4.55 and 5.05, he'd be running long after everyone else was finished. Without self-confidence he would give up before long. However, if he continued racewalking, he would remain in the top group and improve his self-esteem.

My suggestion is to first do something you can do well and that you like doing. That gives you a chance to develop confidence. Establish some short-term goals for yourself. Once you accomplish those you will gain an inner fortitude that will enable you to take on new goals. I suggested that the racewalker continue in order to feel what it's like to excel before starting to run.

Once you succeed at one thing, you have greater strength, which makes it easier to work toward something else. You've got to be realistic about your expectations. It may take years to get to your destination. If you plan your strategy properly, with short-term, intermediate, and long-term goals, you'll be able to note different points in your development. You'll be able to say, "I've really accomplished something." Your progress will be more satisfying if you note improvements along the way.

What expectations do you have of others?

Once you start experiencing success you expect other people to have equal success. You want other people to join you in your success. You're motivated and you want other people to be motivated as well. Your life is happy and you want other people to have a happy life too.

It's fine to want that but, again, your expectations must be realistic. Is the other person capable of doing what you would like her or him to do? Is that what she wants in her life? If not, don't blame her and don't interfere with her life. Accept people for who they are.

One of the worst things you can do is to force your expectations onto another person. A friend of mine contacted me, asking for work. I hired him first because he was a friend in need, and second because he could make a legitimate contribution to my office. He was honest, and told me that because of his addictions he had not worked more than two hours a day for twenty years. He was highly anxious, and explained that because of substance abuse he was hyper, and could only stay focused for short periods of time before looking for distractions. As a result, I suggested he begin by working two hours per day. I felt that to expect more of him than he expected of himself would place immediate stress upon him. Instead, I proposed that he add one hour per day each week, so that by the end of six weeks he would theoretically be working eight-hour days. He agreed to give it a try. At the end of six weeks, he was able to work four hours per day. By some standards, this was a failure. By my standards, this was a partial success. Within nine months he was able to remain sober, drug-free, and not gamble. He had also gone on an exercise and health program, and was attending support group meetings—as well as staying focused on his work.

Look at the people in your life and ask yourself, what are they honestly capable of giving me? That's all you should expect. If they choose to give you more, fine, that's a plus. The point is that having reasonable expectations of people will help you avoid a lot of pain in your life.

Or simply don't ask anything of others. Give without the need to receive. Then you will never be disappointed.

What are the consequences of your thoughts and actions?

There is a consequence to everything you do in life. Do something positive and you'll create a positive result; do something negative and you'll create negativity. If you're bitter and cynical, expect bitter and cynical returns. There's no mystery to this; what you do is self-fulfilling.

Everything you do or say affects someone else at some level. Either you're helping someone or you're causing him harm. If you're not helping someone through your thoughts, actions, and words, *stop* before you affect him in a negative way. Pause and look at the effects you're having on the other person. You have no right to denigrate the human spirit.

If you had only five years left to live, what would you change?

I live my life in five-year cycles. I change entirely every five years, giving up much of what I've accumulated during that time so that I accomplish other things. Only by letting go of things do we have the freedom to move forward and do something else. The problem is we're terrified of what's going to happen if we let go. We're afraid of the high rate of unemployment. In reality, many of the people ultimately beset by unemployment are people who have had ample opportunities to develop alternate careers, skills, and attitudes, but chose not to. While they were working, they never considered the possibility that they could ever lose their jobs. When they lose their jobs, rather than look for opportunities for self-improvement, many of them choose to blame. They sit at home and overeat and are angry. They watch television and wait for someone to come and take them back. They want someone else to be responsible for their working again. That's a welfare mentality. That's saying, I don't want to do it for myself. I want you to do it for me.

What about people who do want to do something for themselves? For every ten people who victimize themselves, I'll show you someone in the same situation who goes out and has a life because he or she has a focus. As long as you have some desire, that desire will motivate you to get a focus, to get an image of what you want.

A sixty-year-old salesperson I knew had burnt himself out. When I asked him, "Where do you want to be?," he said, "I'm sick of the cold climate. I'm sick of all the hustling. I'd like to be in a nice, warm climate where there are positive people who can accept me for just being me."

I suggested that he look into Hawaii. Hawaii is full of adventurous, positive people. It's full of beautiful places to live. It's nice all year round.

He's been there for a couple of years now, and he's as happy as can be. He's managing a surfing show on television. He's not making a lot of money, but he doesn't need it. He's not counting the dollars; he's looking at the happiness. He's in the environment he needs to be in.

For other people, New York might be the perfect environment. It depends upon where you see yourself and what your needs are.

How do others respond to your actions?

There will always be both positive and negative responses to your actions. I spoke with Tony Brown, who had featured me on his TV special on AIDS, about the response to my appearance on the show. He had gotten a lot of positive feedback and some negative reactions as well. One doctor was very angry when he called. "How dare you have Gary Null on the show!" he said. "Where did Gary get those documents? I want those documents. I have a right to those documents." Tony answered, "You don't have a right to anything. Gary got those because he did his homework. Why don't you do yours?"

You see, the doctor was angry because I had held up documents onscreen showing that a person with AIDS had improved using vitamin C drips, ozone therapy, a natural foods diet, juicing, meditation, and guided visualization and prayer, all of which the doctor claimed had no relevance to health. If I hadn't shown the documents, anyone could say the documents didn't exist and keep the AIDS myth going. They could say no cure exists because there's not a shred of evidence that it does. But I had the evidence. Now all they could do was denigrate me for not giving the evidence to them.

Another man called angry about the fact that I wouldn't see him personally about his AIDS. I had spoken with 1800 people. I thought that was enough. If all I do is speak with people all day long, I don't have time to do any of the other things that allow me to help more people. I gave him the names and phone numbers of doctors in his area who could help him, but that's not what he wanted. He wanted hours of my time. But that wasn't reasonable. If he were to call a lawyer and ask for free time, I don't think he would really expect to get it. Since I don't charge people for my time, some people assume it's not worth anything.

What I'm getting at is that you need to act based upon your own convictions, not in response to other people who would have you act to fulfill their personal agendas, which may be in opposition to yours. Do you act in ways that are in accordance with your inner convictions, or do you act to try to please others?

List your assets

You may feel you can't grow because you don't have the necessary resources. You think you can't get out of your rut because you're not capable enough. I say that's not true. You're just unaware of your assets.

To become more aware of what they are, list the assets that allow you to grow, to enjoy life, to engage yourself on all levels, and to make your life happen. Write down your assets in each of the following areas of your life.

Spiritual

What are your spiritual assets? Whenever you have any problem, your spirit helps you to overcome it, to change, to face the crisis. It gives you inner strength more enduring than that supplied by any outside influence. It lets you know that no matter what, you're still okay.

If you acknowledge your spirit, you honor the hero that's inside you. A true hero holds the spirit in high esteem. There's a true sense of sacrifice, not a fear. In battle, people often become heroes, and in sports, athletes with the warrior spirit become heroes. In Somalia volunteer doctors trying to help people are heroes. There's no publicity. They're not doing it for any gain. They're doing it because they're honoring the spirit. And it touches us.

When your spiritual self is guiding you, then everything you do stems from unconditional love. You don't manipulate, lie, or deceive. You don't do anything that dishonors the human spirit and hence you don't dishonor other people. There is no hidden agenda.

Getting in touch with the hero inside you allows the best part of your nature to emerge. You instantly know what is real and true. One of the ways to grow is to honor the inner spirit—the warrior, the hero, the healer. Every human being has it. So acknowledge it, let it out, and discover that suddenly you're a different human being because you don't face adversity in the old way. Panic, desperation, overreaction, anger, and anxiety leave. Instead you can deal with life and every problem that arises. You keep your balance. You're confident that you're going to be okay no matter what. That spiritual component is an important asset. Use it.

Intellectual

What are your intellectual assets? Your intellect is what allows you to reason, to look at all aspects of an issue, and thus to find solutions to problems. Intellect gives you the ability to discern choices and the judgment to value certain choices over others. It provides you with perspective so that you don't have to feel overwhelmed. You can choose to do something in a way that is reasonable considering your needs.

Emotional

List your emotional assets. Can you express your emotions to other people? Do you understand your own emotions? Healthy emotions are accompanied by an understanding of what you're feeling. You might, for instance, feel upset every time someone questions you. Instead of reacting to your emotion stop yourself and ask, "Where does this emotion come from? Why is it every time this happens I feel this way?" If you don't get in touch with what you're feeling, you might find yourself repeating an undesirable pattern of behavior.

Educational

Most people assume that their education is what they've learned in school. But formal schooling is relatively insignificant. Most of what you learn in school has nothing to do with whether you succeed in life. Most schools don't teach the important lessons, such as interpersonal communication, problem solving, conflict resolution, and critical thinking. You learn these lessons in life, and they are critical to your wellbeing. Quite simply, everyone has gained some unique skills, knowledge, or insights from their education. These can be used to your advantage. Don't downplay them.

Location

Look at the assets your location has to offer. Many people, for instance, downplay New York. A woman sitting next to me on a flight from Texas hated New York and told me everything wrong with it—the crime and violence, for instance. I told her she was both right and wrong. Yes, there is crime, but every city in America has crime. And there's violence everywhere too. What she neglected to notice was that New York has better career opportunities than any other place in America. There are also some beautiful environments in New York and many wonderful people. There are more museums than in any other place on earth. All of these assets, plus New York's uniqueness, color, and vitality are the reasons I choose to live there.

Think about where you live. What are its assets? And do you take advantage of them?

How have you used your assets to enhance your life?

Have you ever asked yourself, what is the best that I can be? Have you ever pictured yourself without any constraints, moving beyond what you now think is possible? You can't undo your limitations to a certain degree. You either shed your limitations or you don't.

Make a note to yourself that starting tomorrow you're going to create the ideal self, the ideal job, and the ideal relationship. Maybe you have it all now. If you do, fine. Then honor it. If you don't, then gather up all your assets, focus on your ideal self, and work toward what you want.

Honoring Your Assets

With every asset comes a responsibility that you must honor. You honor your assets by using them. Each day that you don't use an asset, you weaken yourself. This morning, for example, I did a speed workout along the Central Park Reservoir even though there was a 37 degree below-zero wind chill factor. Why? My physical fitness is an asset, I honor it, and I want to keep using it—daily. (By the way, when you start moving, your body warms up, so that five minutes into a speed workout you can be sweating. In many cases what you might anticipate to be problematic—in this instance the cold—turns out not to be a problem at all.)

Create a plan to increase your assets and decrease your liabilities

Notice the liabilities that keep showing up in your life—fear, lack of time, anger. How might you limit these? The first step is to know what you don't want in your life. If people keep wasting your time, for example, you can simply let them know how they make you feel by saying, "Sorry, I don't have time to give you."

You can overcome your own fears by facing them head on. You'll find that most of your fears stem from your imagination more than from reality.

For example, many people fear financial failure. But if you envision the worst that could possibly happen, you can dissipate that fear. Does losing what you have change you as a person? I know people who live on ashrams or other retreats for periods of their lives, with no material possessions whatsoever, to better understand their spirituality. They own nothing. They eat a frugal diet and sleep on mats in a communal room. These people give up everything to practice techniques that enhance their spiritual awareness. When they feel a renewed inner strength that connects them to a larger vision of life, they go back into the world. What these people find is that what they have in the world is not as important as knowing who they are.

People in the most economically distressed circumstances can live a completely fulfilling life. I would rather have a fulfilling life that allows me to feel good about myself as a person than to have financial or material security. Of course, this attitude requires taking risks.

I met a man on the street who came from a Wall Street background. He said that one day he found himself homeless because he had waited too long to change. After he lost his job, he waited and waited to get rehired. He used up all his money and wasn't able to pay his mortgage. His friends and family stopped lending him money. One day he came home and his door was locked. They had taken all of his belongings. Everything he had feared, everything he had worked so hard to keep from happening, happened in that instant.

He spent three days on the street in a state of shock. He wouldn't go to a shelter even for food.

On the fourth day he thought, "What the heck am I doing? I've got a mind." He started going through garbage and recycling things. He got giant garbage bags and did ten times the recycling of anybody else. From this he made $60 a day. He was able to do that seven days a week and earn $420, which is more than most people in America take home.

He was able to get back on his feet. In two months he had a small apartment. He started a home-based business, and began attending night school. Now he has a whole new career. Ironically, it's the career he had always wanted but was afraid he couldn't do.

Now he's not afraid of losing what he has because when the bottom fell out he still survived. He's a stronger person for what he went through. He realizes that when things fall apart they happen for a reason. On Wall Street he hadn't been content with his life and had needed to change. But he'd been afraid to let go, to take risks. He was living by his fear, not his strength. Now he has a life he enjoys.

Ask yourself if you hold on to old ways that no longer serve you because of fear? Are you able to let go and trust that something new and better will replace the old? Once again, look at your assets. Notice what you are capable of doing and focus on that instead of on your fears. Life is as self-fulfilling as you imagine it.

Create both short- and long-term goals

Goals help you to become more balanced and whole because they give you a sense of purpose and direction. You become engaged in the process of your life.

You should have both long-term and short-term goals. The long-term goals should be slightly beyond your reach; the short-term goals should be those you can attain if you keep your sense of focus.

Give yourself one week to create a short-term goal. Each day, take time to create your plan. Use the input you receive here as well as from the many other resources you have. What you learn only becomes meaningful when actualized.

Then create a long-term goal. When I write a book I don't just wake up one morning and jot down the entire thing off the top of my head. I start with a plan of action. One project can take me two to three years to complete. Research and planning take time and patience, but I know that as long as I keep focused, I can do it.

You must be willing to acknowledge that you will make errors. You'll fall off track at times. We all do that. As long as you get back on track, you'll be alright.

Do you become excited by the possibility of change but fail to actualize it?

You may think you are ready to change but never actually take action. You make excuses instead. You are going to start a diet tomorrow. You're prepared to throw out all the sugar, meat, caffeine, and everything else that's bad for you. Then you think maybe you shouldn't get rid of it. After all, it cost you seventeen dollars.

Forget the seventeen dollars! You have to do something each day to affirm your commitment to change and one of the easiest things for you to do is toss away all the bad food. Select a goal for the day in the area that you specifically want to change. When you wake up in the morning, the very first thing you need to do is work out a strategy to achieve that goal, whatever it is. Write it down. Work toward that goal every single day, seven days a week. That helps you to focus on what you need to do for yourself.

Make that one small goal the focal point of your day. Make everything else secondary. Your goal becomes your reason for waking up in the morning. That motivation will help you achieve what you want.

At the end of the week you will have achieved seven minor goals, and at the end of the month, 28 to 31. In one month, three months, six months, and one year you can achieve goals of increasing magnitude. In a year's time you will have accomplished a life goal, as well as 365 minor goals, 12 important goals, four major goals, and two long-range goals. Think of it: all of this in just a year, by concentrating on one thing per day.

Once you achieve your goal, don't take a step backward. If your goal for the day is to not have sugar, don't have sugar. This is not unrealistic if you are concerned only with honoring your body and mind. You're establishing new priorities. In effect, you're starting life over with the issues that you want to focus on and the ideals you want to create. Since you're the architect of this new scheme, you're going to honor it.

If you should fall back, don't beat yourself up over it. Analyze what went wrong. Do something nice for yourself such as going to a movie, taking a walk, meeting friends, or cooking yourself a special dinner. Reward yourself for being human, but in a positive way.

To what do you feel naturally connected?

When you feel naturally connected to what you are doing, the activity comes easily to you. Honor that feeling. In other words, realize that where passion and excitement are is where your life should be. If your passion is helping people and your career doesn't offer that, then take the time to learn the necessary skills to make a career change.

If you follow your natural passion and excitement, you will automatically know what you want to do with your life. I'm willing to bet that, inside of you, a voice has told you a million times what you really want. It's tried to draw you to the real self through feelings and fantasies, but getting in the way of your accepting those were a lot of other images, e.g., you had to be the family man or wife, the responsible member of society, or the successful professional person, when perhaps these weren't you at all.

I'm not suggesting for a second some radical detachment from life as you know it. I'm not asking that you push a significant part of yourself into a guillotine. Rather, I'm suggesting that you think about preparing yourself over a period of time for what is real, new, and essential. This will allow you to extend one energy forward and at the same time retract the other energy. At some point—in one, two, or three years— you'll be fully into your new life and the old life will be gone. The process should be gradual as you do what is natural and healthy at a pace that is natural and healthy.

List the things you feel naturally attracted to. For example, what makes you feel excited, interested, and passionate? If these feelings persist and your interest grows even more, then this is your inner self sending you messages to follow your bliss. It's not important whether you are educated or even skilled in the area. That can always come later. Alongside list the things you feel pressured to accept and the things that feel unnatural and intuitively wrong so that you can start to disengage from those things. I call this constructive disengagement; it's constructively letting go of the things that are not a part of your natural self. Look at what you have made yourself responsible for that feels artificial, and constructively disengage.

Be prepared to be judged and rejected

Be firm about what you are doing even in the face of objections and rejections from others. Before I go into a meeting, I try to anticipate most of the objections that are going to hit me and I prepare answers for them in advance.

For example, recently I gave my publisher a book I wanted published that wasn't a part of my contractual obligation, knowing in advance that he would say "Well, you know Gary, this isn't. . . ." I had already anticipated his negative response and had answers prepared that would justify publishing the book. After I answered all his objections, there was a turnaround. They will be publishing my book. Had I not prepared for his objections in advance, my book would not be on its way to publication.

When you believe in something, be affirmative about it. Hear a "yes" in your mind even before you start the conversation. Think of possible reasons that people will have for rejecting your ideas, and build into your plan an answer to every possible rejection. Otherwise, people's disapproval may kill your ideas before they get off the ground. If you do your homework, there will be little room for rejection.

There is no final destination

Do you believe that at some point you arrive at your final destination? Or do you understand that you never arrive but continue your journey after each brief interlude when you reach a new goal?

Most people think their goals will get them to a certain fixed point in life. At that point, they assume, they will no longer need to grow. A doctorate or a master's degree will prove they are smart and can stop studying. A job, a bonus, or a pension, will mean that they have made it.

When people reach a goal they often try to build a protective barrier around themselves to keep the world out and prevent any further changes. Their attainments become a fortress. This is akin, though, to taking free-flowing water into a pool: The pool remains clear for a day or two but soon becomes a cesspool and dies. Our life putrefies in the same way when we remove ourselves from the flow of life.

You have to set new sights and move on. It's fine to pat yourself on the back to acknowledge yourself for attaining some long-sought-after goal, but life does go on. It's a continual journey.

My life is always changing. I'll be altering a major segment of my life over the next few months. I'm going to have a lot of new and exciting things happen that will enable me to reach a lot more people. But to do that I have to live by my philosophy of never taking on a new project until I give up an old one. Think of what would happen if you did the same thing.

I worked very hard to establish the first holistic gourmet natural foods restaurant in New York City. It was called the Fertile Earth. I had it for five years. Then I opened another restaurant called Gary's Place. It had great food that was beautifully presented. I hired a French decorative chef whose only job was to decorate each dish before it came out of the kitchen. Every single dish looked like a work of art. In fact, people couldn't believe basic dishes could be so beautiful, and yet remain inexpensive as well.

Then one day I was asked to do a television show. It wouldn't pay anything. In fact, it would cost me $100,000. But I would be able to reach a lot more people with my message. I agreed to do it.

The next day, I sold my restaurant. It was that simple. I needed to move forward and in order to start a new project I had to let go of an old one. If someone else wanted to carry on what I had started, that would be fine. If the public is aware of what you're doing and feels a need for what you've created, they'll carry it on. Otherwise, it has had its time. Life is a matter of things coming and going. Some things stay and get carried on; others don't.

I did 165 television programs that aired in Connecticut, New Jersey, and Massachusetts for six years. That served a purpose. Then I started another project and gave up the television show. The idea is to start something, do it, enjoy it, and then let go and do something else. This directly contradicts the popular idea of finding your niche and holding on to something for the rest of your life. Where is it written that you have to spend your life doing just one thing? You can do many things in your life—as long as you don't do too many things at once.

Don't take what you do too seriously. Just know that everything you do is the best that you can do. Even if what you do isn't as good as you would like it to be, know that if you strive a little more you will do better. You're not striving out of anxiety or fear. You're not working for ego gratification. You're not trying to gain approval from the world to prove to other people that you're alright. You're doing it as part of a natural process of growth. Watch a horse run in a pasture. The horse is not running in order to win a trophy. It's running for the joy of running. It's natural to run. We forget to do what is natural, to honor our natural energies.

You may not know your goal until you've reached it

Sometimes you don't know what your goal is. You may think you've reached it when in fact you're only at an interim stopping-off point on a longer journey to a very different kind of goal.

For example, my good friend George, whom I grew up with, seemed to have it all at one point. He was the very successful manager of an advertising agency. He had an upscale house in the suburbs, and a beautiful wife and children. However, it had all come too easily. He'd seemed to have succeeded on the basis of his personal charm and ability to inspire trust. Because he was likeable and somewhat glib, he'd managed to do well financially, but there was something hollow about his life.

George became a gambler, dropping vast sums of money and jeopardizing his family's savings. He also became an alcoholic and a drug addict. He was diabetic as well; in short, not in good shape. Despite all his problems, and despite the fact that these were keeping him away from work for days at a time, he was able to hang on to his job for almost three years, mainly by force of his compelling personality.

Yet he was spinning downhill all this time, and when the company changed hands, George finally lost his job. He soon found himself in a halfway house, working in a chair factory.

I hadn't seen George during this downhill period, and when I met up with him when I was in town for our thirtieth high school reunion, I was alarmed by how awful he looked. He was puffy-faced, overweight, haggard, smoking. At the reunion I noticed how our cohorts' smiles of greeting to George turned to disapproving frowns as soon as he walked away. He'd been in town for a month before the reunion and many people knew his story. People have difficulty looking compassionately at golden-boy types who self-destruct.

Shortly after the reunion, I went over to George's and asked him, "Do you want to get out of this stagnant recovering-alcoholic, recovering-drug-addict thing?" "Sure," he said. So I arranged for George to visit my ranch to learn about health and nutrition, and to revamp his habits. He did this, and for the first time in years, George began to wake up each morning with joy in his heart.

Then he came to visit me in New York. He had a positive attitude and was appreciative of everything new and exciting the city had to offer. There was just one problem. George didn't know how to be politically correct! He's the type that tends to say what's on his mind, and he's not sensitive to boundaries. In a city where keeping your distance is practically an art form, George offended people fairly regularly.

He knew that he and New York City were a mismatch. The upshot of all this is that George has gone back to the ranch, this time to work helping others who are going through personal crises involving drug addiction, relationships, or other problems. His personality attributes—the ones that kept him going in his advertising job—are being used in a modified, more humane way, in a counseling capacity.

George has reinvented his life. He's a wonderful, totally honest human being who is motivated by the joy of living. He's a sensitive and compassionate listener. He knows how to make each day work because he's learned many lessons by living them.

The Chinese have a proverb—"To travel far you must travel light"—and George, who has shed a lot of the material trappings of his earlier "successful" life, is an inspiring example of this.

Being Autonomous

MOST PEOPLE DON'T DECIDE WHETHER OR NOT TO PURSUE THEIR dreams. They consult other people and wait for their approval. If their ideas are rejected, chances are they'll give up their dreams rather than oppose the people who advised against it. Even if they go ahead and do what they want, they allow the influence of other people to make them feel fearful and guilty. They don't approach their dream with an open heart and mind, and this breaks the flow of energy.

You generally consult the same people for support, advice, and acceptance. So in time, you begin to know in advance what these people will accept or reject and, as a result, you begin to edit your thoughts. You don't share real feelings, desires, and ambitions. Instead, you say only what you think the people want to hear. That way, you will be accepted.

But what happens to the part of you that no one knows about? It becomes secret. In time, it can manifest as a pathology.

When you betray yourself by neglecting to honor your dreams, you lose control of your life. You let someone else get into the driver's seat and control your life. You can change that, however, by identifying which people you seek permission from and asking, why do I need their blessing?

Do what's important to you. You might explain your intent to others, out of courtesy, but keep in mind that only you know what is best for you. You are going to go through with your decision whether anyone else supports you or not. Hopefully, some of these people will comprehend what you need to do for yourself. If they don't understand, they are entitled to their feelings, but you don't have to accept them.

Paradigms can blind us to possibilities

A thirty-year-old professional woman admitted to me that she had had many relationships but that none of them had been fulfilling. She decided that she would like to be freer but still be part of a relationship. The question was, how do you combine the two? Either you belong to a relationship and are devoted to your partner, or you are free. At least that is the model set forth by our society; a relationship in which you *are* free is not generally viewed as an option. This woman is not the only person with this quandary. Many people are dissatisfied with the standard sort of relationship they are taught they need in order to be happy. Yet they stick with what they are taught, and stop short at looking at other possibilities.

The same holds true in other areas of life. Your mind is conditioned to react in specific ways, thus eliminating your internal reasoning. You learn to shape your reality around being Catholic, Jewish, Islamic, Republican, Democratic, and so on, and to take on all the trappings of that identity. You accept or reject information because you are expected to respond to it in a certain fashion, not because you feel it is inherently right or wrong.

You become attached to the facade you create—a personality, a persona, an ideology, a religion—in order to feel more comfortable and safe in the world. While belonging helps you adapt to the circumstances of your existence, it doesn't help you to transform your life. You may, for instance, choose to live in an area that's flooded or burned down year after year instead of moving to safer ground. What keeps you there? What keeps you in the same predictable patterns leading to the same results every single time?

To understand your behavior, you have to appreciate the power of the paradigm. Paradigm comes from the Greek, paradigma, meaning pattern. Picture a circle inside of which all your needs are supposed to be met, and every question you have is supposed to be answered. That's what societal paradigms attempt to do. Let me be more specific. Belief systems are the central catalysts of every part of society. Most groups try to centralize their power, and reward those who honor their belief system, while punishing and excluding those who disagree, and in general exhibiting a very low tolerance for change in any of the fundamental beliefs.

A major example of this would be in medicine. Doctors are taught what is considered the scientific basis of medical practice, the assumption being that they are the sole experts on the cause and treatment of any condition from heart disease to AIDS. As a result, medical organizations have, for more than fifty years, fought a protracted war against cancer—and with few exceptions, have failed miserably. In such instances, protocol often becomes more important than the patient. If, however, you're on the other side of the medical paradigm, it's easy to see how doctors have gone in the wrong direction by looking for a viral cause of cancer, rather than expanding research into multifactorial causes—environment, diet, and behavior—all of which can be changed. But because the paradigm of the medical belief system has excluded these factors as "unscientific," there's no chance that serious research will be funded. As a result, vast amounts of money continue to be spent in search of an elusive virus, while the bodies mount up —over 500,000 per year. Paradigms that include alternatives, such as diet, herbs, vitamin C drips, and that recognize the culpability of ozone levels, have shown enormous benefit in both prevention and treatment—while being derided by the medical establishment as not being "real science." Truth in science, then, is determined by who controls the power base; and until their minds are opened to new ideas and asking new questions, nothing will change. So, to the degree by which you are directed by an institutional belief system, your reality, perceptions, and truth will be merely an extension of theirs. They serve as models for behavior and thought—e.g., the relationship model, or paradigm, of the woman I spoke with was one of interdependence and lack of freedom.

You may know the paradigms you've internalized are inherently wrong but lack the confidence to challenge them. You may listen to my radio show and read my books, for example, yet run to a standard doctor at the first sign of sickness. You are afraid to trust your feelings. Instead you adhere to the paradigm that you were conditioned to accept. You accept that traditional medicine has the only true solutions.

I've been curious for a long time about many of life's contradictions. In the area of medicine we say that we want to do anything possible to alleviate suffering. Yet when someone comes up with a new and innovative idea that helps people, and that certainly would help more people if given wider exposure, it is immediately attacked because it is outside the accepted paradigm. So benefits people claim to be receiving are completely ignored.

On the other hand, the scientific community condones ideas that have not produced successful responses from patients. Dr. Robert Gallo of the National Institutes of Health decided in 1984 that the cause of AIDS was a single retrovirus called HIV. That theory became dogma overnight. If you want to get a grant for AIDS research, you have to accept that HIV is the cause. So an enormous industry has emerged around the virus.

Nowhere in medical history have anomalies been more apparent. Look at the following contradictions:

- People are told that AIDS is a highly infectious disease that will reach epidemic proportions throughout the world. But when you step away from the hysteria and look at the actual statistics of people with proven AIDS, as opposed to people with AIDS-like symptoms who actually have malaria or TB, you can see that the disease remains mainly in its original risk groups of fast-track homosexuals, hemophiliacs, and IV-drug-using heterosexuals.

- People are told to wear condoms to keep AIDS from spreading. But condoms only prevent bacterial sexually transmitted microbes from being transferred. They do nothing to prevent viruses, such as HIV, from passing through latex. Viruses are smaller than the pores of the latex.

- People are told that they will die within fourteen to eighteen months of being infected. Yet people have been living with AIDS for fourteen or fifteen years.

- People are told that AIDS has a long latency period. That defies all scientific logic. There is no known virus that can destroy the entire immune system, create 29 separate diseases, and be latent for indefinite periods of time.

- People are told that the mere presence of HIV antibodies will cause AIDS to manifest. Yet antibodies are known to protect and immunize people against disease. This is true with polio, measles, mumps, smallpox, and chickenpox. This is the first time the presence of antibodies means that you are going to get the disease and die. There is no basis for this in science.

People who best survive AIDS use alternative therapies. They change their diets and lifestyles, use vitamin C drips, ozone treatments, vitamins, juices, and homeopathic and herbal therapies to cleanse and strengthen their immune systems. People often become HIV-negative after adhering to these protocols for a period of time. And even if they test positive for HIV, their blood is normal in all other aspects.

Society tends to ignore these success stories. When I held a press conference in New York City, the room was full of people who had been diagnosed with advanced AIDS. They chose holistic treatments and were able to reverse their condition. At the time of the conference, these people were healthy, with normal blood chemistries.

Every major news organization in the country was invited to attend, but not a single one showed up. If I had been presenting a drug that kills viruses in a test tube, it would have been a different scenario. Everyone would have been there and the story would have made front-page news. But the media weren't interested in stories about people triumphing over the disease process without the aid of conventional medicine. The information fell outside the accepted paradigm.

I had the identical experience years ago when I held a press conference to introduce survivors of inoperable cancers. Five, ten, and twenty years after diagnosis these people were completely cured. I had medical records showing the original diagnoses and reports verifying how well they were doing. But all this didn't seem to matter. No one in the media paid any attention to the event.

I've seen other successful modalities ignored as well. Dr. Marshall Mandell was censured for curing upwards of eighty-five percent of his arthritic patients with rotational diets and detoxification programs. Doctors using chelation therapy, vitamins, and changes in diet have high success rates curing heart patients. But their work and patients are ignored and the doctors are attacked.

I've also seen contradictions occur outside of medicine. Look at the following examples:

- People are told to be innovative and work for themselves. Bureaucratic rules and regulations, however, make it almost impossible for most people to open their own businesses.

- Candidates for government office often proclaim a need for campaign reform. They say it's unfair that only the very rich are able to buy enough air time to get elected. Candidates should not be allowed to use private funds, they claim; they should all be given an equal amount of money and media time. That way, just normal, average people will have a chance to be elected to office. But the moment these people are elected to office, they stop being interested in campaign reform.

- People in the media claim to be working in the public interest, yet they're constantly selling the public everything from alcohol to cigarettes, and providing them with violent programming.

Everywhere I look I see discrepancies between what people say and what they do.

One of the problems is that no matter what we think, we are part of a belief system that determines our reality. Let's return to the field of medicine. If you're a physician, you have been trained to believe that medicine should be practiced in a certain way. You're given a standard set of rules about what causes disease, and you're given a standard set of tools with which to treat it. Society rewards you with social acceptance, financial security, and public trust when you follow the canon.

Here is the irony. If you use the therapies you're instructed to use and every patient you have dies, you are still rewarded. No one questions your choice of treatment. You are not held accountable. The protocol, then, is more important than the patient. The patient is there to serve medicine's larger ideology.

Patients tend to look up to their physicians and to believe what they are told. They are expected to be submissive. Obedience on the part of the patient is crucial for the system to continue, and people are taught to respect those in charge. Even when they know the authority is wrong they tend not to want to offend them.

When a patient voices uncertainty by questioning a therapy —"Can you show me five cases of people who have been cured with this technique?"—the doctor will try to put the patient back in his place. "This is your only hope," he might say. If a patient continues to inquire about holistic options, the doctor will try to intimidate the patient into accepting standard methods. He will say, at best, that alternatives are unproven and regarded as ineffective. This is intended to discourage the patient from pursuing other possibilities and to keep the patient from losing confidence in the system.

This does not mean that the doctor doesn't care about his or her patients. It means that he is being guided by a certain set of beliefs. The doctor's psyche is indoctrinated with the idea that anything that is not part of the system must be rejected. His immediate reaction to anything foreign is to call it quackery. If it were legitimate, he thinks, he would know about it. It would be written up in medical journals. Researchers would test it and doctors would talk about it. After all, he reasons, doctors want to see a cure for cancer. Their daughters, sons, wives, and parents get cancer too. If the doctor doesn't know about it, it must not be valid.

Think again. People with vested interests in maintaining paradigms hate to be challenged. Look at the following scenario:

A doctor sees patients getting well after going on a detoxification and stress management program. These patients make changes in diet, drink fresh vegetable juices, eat raw foods, and take large amounts of selenium, vitamin C, and other nutrients.

The doctor realizes, "My God! I've been doing it all wrong. This patient is not sick because of a gene or virus. He has an immunosuppressive disorder. He's been living under chronic stress in a toxic environment and eating a poor diet. Clearly all these poisons are accumulating and causing cancer."

Now the doctor understands how a person can progress toward wellness. He no longer sees disease as a noun, a cancer, but as a verb, or a process. The doctor is excited and talks to his colleagues about his findings.

Also, if alternative treatments help patients, then standard therapies and medications become suspect. They may be causing symptoms that get confused with the symptoms of an illness. It's difficult to differentiate characteristics caused by a disease from those caused by medication. In the case of AIDS or cancer, symptoms caused by chemotherapy become confused with those caused by the AIDS or cancer. In a depressed patient on medication, suicidal behavior might be related to the patient's depression or it might be medically induced.

In short, it's not in the best interest of the status quo to allow doctors to dissent from the norm, especially when the dissenters are getting good results. These doctors must follow the rules or be punished.

Thus doctors who praise, use, and research unorthodox approaches are first warned to stop. If they choose not to listen, they are admonished more strongly. Further persistence results in the doctor being isolated from the medical community altogether. The doctor will lose his or her privileges at the hospital, and will no longer be allowed to publish in peer review journals, or obtain research grants.

What happened to Dr. Peter Duesberg is a good example of this. Dr. Duesberg was considered a golden boy of American science, one of the best retrovirologists, and a scientific genius until he had the boldness to suggest that the HIV does not cause AIDS. Although he gave very plausible explanations and backed up his statements with good scientific reasoning, he was excluded from the scientific community for his outspokeness. His funding dried up and his teaching was restricted even though he taught at a supposed bastion of intellectual enlightenment, the University of California at Berkeley.

There are many doctors right now who are losing their licenses. A lot of these physicians had stellar reputations in the medical community until they began incorporating into their practices approaches to treatment that were not part of the accepted medical model—approaches that, ironically, earned these doctors the reputation of quacks even as they were helping patients and eliminating iatrogenic (medical-treatment-induced) problems. So these doctors now wake up every day knowing that the other 600,000 practicing doctors in this country will not come to their support no matter how many cures they can show and how many successful cases they have. Instead, they will be thrown out of the establishment, proving the old saying that no good deed goes unpunished.

Why, when they're successful helping their patients, are these doctors being selected for chastisement? If they used standard treatments they'd be hurting their patients. On the one hand, this scenario doesn't make any sense. On the other hand, it's easy to understand if you remember the power inherent in belief systems and when you realize that there's nothing more threatening in any belief system than an idea that cannot be controlled.

Once on the outside, doctors are able to see, more objectively, the limitations and false notions of the belief systems they participated in at one time. If they are able to move forward, they become the pioneers in a new system of medicine and are able to look at old problems with an open mind and a new point of view. So the doctors getting the best results treating AIDS patients are not part of the orthodoxy. The scientists doing the most to understand its cause are not looking at HIV. They are looking at multifactorial causes, such as drug use, repeated unhealthy sexual acts, and chronic abuse of the immune system. These doctors who have stepped back from the medical "party line," if you will, are able to be more objective and are therefore better able to help patients.

Society accepts only one ruling system. Even though various people uphold that power, they represent the same set of principles. It's like being the president of the United States—it doesn't matter whether you're Democratic or Republican. There is really only one party—the business party—and both groups honor the business mandate. That's not necessarily good or bad, but it's the reality.

Another contradiction: We say that we want equality, yet we don't encourage it. We say that people have the same opportunities, yet people in positions of power never let others get a taste of it. We almost never see wealthy people associating with the poor, educated people befriending illiterate people, people fraternizing with people of other races or even other age groups.

Our statements are politically correct but practically void. We don't acknowledge the apparent contradictions and inconsistencies in all areas of our life. We don't take things in the larger context. We don't see the consequences of our actions. We don't visualize a larger way of living. Then we wonder why nothing gets better.

How do paradigms function?

Paradigms prescribe values. You learn to care about things you are constantly told to believe are important. For instance, our culture endorses a paradigm that encourages spending, along with the creation of artificial needs. People are taught to continually buy, in order to support the "supply side" of our economic system. If you don't have the means, you can still buy on credit. You can buy fashionable clothes and dispose of the ones your paradigm tells you are too old and no longer stylish. You need new clothes in order to feel good, the fashion industry says.

There's nothing wrong with feeling good or with having nice things to wear. The problem lies in your being made to feel you always need something new to feel good. You then begin to devalue what you liked at one time. So you have fifteen pair of shoes but wear only two. You have twenty dresses but wear three. If you lived in France you would have four dresses and wear all four. The French save until they can afford something they really like, while the United States is a society of disposables. It's all part of our economic paradigm.

People defend their paradigms even when they're harmful. A good example of this phenomenon is the issue of smoking. It was profitable to start people smoking, and the cigarette industry worked hard at it. They even paid doctors to promote smoking's supposed safety on television. Doctors would say that cigarettes were safe according to scientific studies. People felt comforted by that, because if their doctor said smoking was alright, it had to be so. As a result, smoking became an acceptable part of their paradigm. If they later got emphysema, people were caught in a paradox. Did they trust their own experience or the doctor's message? Often they might trust their doctor and not their own experience, since a physician signifies authority.

Paradigm followers also tend to blame people outside of their own belief system for problems that arise instead of questioning their own beliefs. So conservatives attack liberals, liberals attack conservatives, Democrats attack Republicans, and so on. The problem is always the outsiders—never the insiders' assumptions.

Belief systems tend to establish a wall of accepted thought beyond which you must not venture. Orthodoxy tells you to stop all your questioning at this wall. That's because those who have an interest in maintaining certain points of view must discourage you from questioning, since if you investigated the beliefs you've been fed, the likelihood is that you would go beyond them as you found their weaknesses. You would start to see the paradigm's limitations and say to yourself, "Hold on a second. I can't accept this."

How do you work outside of a paradigm?

Realistically, you'll probably need to find a way to work within the existing paradigm while taking care that your beliefs are not compromised. You can't just change everything about your society but you can change your part in it. For example if you feel uncomfortable with your work routine, you could start a business from your home, as an alternative to fitting into somebody else's nine-to-five framework.

I recently spoke with someone about a magnificent business he started. He said to me, "Gary, I've got a great business and I want you to tell people in New York because maybe they can do the same thing. Everyone is interested in health and looking for an easy way of maintaining it. To help them, I've made up a menu of juices. I make fresh juice each day and go around to corporations, businesses, and restaurants, where I sell it in containers. It's easier and quicker for people than if they made it themselves, and it gives me a nice income. I enjoy this work because it allows me to offer something healthful to society. I'm doing something good that I like and making some money in the process. Plus I'm maintaining my autonomy by setting my own hours and working for myself. Sometimes I work longer than I would in a nine-to-five job, but I don't mind because I'm working for me."

What a great idea. And this is just one of a million ideas that are coming to light in America right now. People are actualizing their ideas. If you're creative you can come to grips with any problem. Instead of adapting to a bad circumstance transform it to work for you. How much better this is than escaping and running away from things you don't like.

Does authority limit you?

Authority exists everywhere. It influences every aspect of your life. You consult a counselor before making a career change. You see a doctor to determine whether you're healthy.

Established experts act as if they're the only credible source. In our health care system, for example, people who suggest you can be healthy with the aid of yoga, meditation, tai chi, wheat grass, or guided visualization are disempowered by the mainstream, and you're discouraged from seeking advice from them. Their charges are not covered by health insurance. The media ignores them or makes them look laughable. The scientific community overlooks them, and they're not given academic acceptance.

Most authorities are concerned with self-preservation. Therefore, they are limited in what they can tell you. You may speak to a hundred experts but if they've all bought into the same paradigm, you're hearing the same words from a hundred different mouths. This doesn't mean that authorities from the prevailing paradigm are bad people or that they don't want to help. It just means they may be limited in the aid they can offer and in the information they can accept.

A highly regarded physician called me. He told me he is suffering from AIDS and cancer and from the side effects of chemotherapy. I asked him if anyone could assure him that the chemotherapy was going to work. He explained that he had no assurance. I suggested that he try a protocol that would build the immune system rather than destroy it. He said he couldn't because he is an orthodox doctor.

This doctor is a victim of his own limited beliefs. He refuses to try something new even in the face of life-threatening illnesses. That's how powerful belief systems are. That's how authority limits you. A reasonable argument could be made to the effect of: Why would the doctor call me and ask for my advice if he had no intention of using it? This happens all the time. My assumption is that by at least calling he was assuaging some guilt for not having looked into everything. But looking and learning about a therapy is not the same as engaging in it. He was keeping it on a linear, left-brain, very safe analytical level, and I would suppose that if someone asked him, "Have you even looked into alternative therapy?" he could say, "I called Gary Null, I even spend time listening to him. I just wasn't convinced that what he had to offer would work."

You need to be the authority in your life. Go after what you really need.

What if you broke out of an accepted pattern?

Let's say you've decided to be single at a stage in life when this is not quite the thing to do. Being unpaired often threatens people who are paired. If you enjoy being alone you may become a threat to people who derive security and meaning from being in relationships. When you are no longer married, notice how quickly most other married people exclude you from their lives. You may have been friends before but now, no matter what you've shared, suddenly you're out of the loop.

I've counseled numerous people confused about why no one wants them around once they're single again. Sometimes the reason is jealousy. A single person's lifestyle is different and often more engaging. They have freedom that their married friends can't relate to. Most married people don't want to hear about a fun party or an exciting rafting expedition if their life has no place for those. They don't like to acknowledge something that they can't share.

Is fear of losing acceptance holding you back from being more independent? Or do you have faith that you will meet new like-minded people? Are you able to let go of the old, if necessary, so that you can live a more self-empowered life?

How do you hide your loneliness or sense of not belonging?

As a society we believe that we must belong to something, so we tend to join different groups. We identify with these groups. There's nothing wrong with that, provided we don't lose our own identity. We shouldn't use groups to hide our loneliness.

Since you were taught that you must be connected to something to feel whole, when you're not connected you tend to feel isolated and abandoned. Sometimes it's hard for people to cope with this sense of abandonment. But remember that aloneness is not synonymous with loneliness. Think of the things you can do alone. You can meditate, relax, do things for yourself, and have time to put your life in order. Quality time alone can give you a much needed new perspective. In this chaotic world, where everything seems to require our time, isn't it nice to have time alone?

When you choose to be with people, make sure your time is spent with people you enjoy. Don't seek company just so you won't feel lonely. That isn't enjoying the company. That's hiding from the loneliness. If I'm with someone it's because I choose to be with the person, not because I'm lonely. If I'm with someone just because I'm lonely, then I'm not really accepting or appreciating that person. She or he is merely the means I use to help me overcome my loneliness, and that's devaluing to us both.

What are the advantages of being single or married?

Whether you're single or married, list the best parts of the experience and the worst. Then ask yourself an honest question. Do you feel good about your status? Does your life work? Are you happy?

Maybe you are unhappy being single only because your conditioning tells you that you should be married at your age. Your friends and parents pressure you to meet someone or to get more serious in your relationship. You really like being alone but this is unacceptable to others.

Perhaps you are unhappily married and feel pressured to make it work. In your heart you know you would prefer being on your own.

You may, on the other hand, be happily married. If being married makes your life work more successfully, that's fine.

Being single or married is not, in itself, good or bad. Acknowledging your true feelings and honest needs is what's important. Make a list of these. This list will help you create balance.

How do you respond to uncertainty?

Making changes in your life will undoubtedly lead to feelings of uncertainty. If uncertainty makes you uncomfortable your first reaction will be to avoid unpleasant feelings. You might back away, scurry into a relationship, or keep chronically busy. Then you're never going to get around to projecting your new self. You're always going to find something else that's a priority.

When you feel uncertain, you may revert to childlike behavior. You might feel you need to be taken care of or to be told what and how to do something. A sense of abandonment and rejection can keep you in an unhealthy situation, even an abusive one. You may resort to childish behavior out of a misguided desire to be needed and accepted.

Notice how you respond to uncertainties. If you respond in unhealthy ways you can work to change that.

Where do you go to have your needs met?

You'll almost always go to the people inside of your paradigm for answers. A problem arises when your needs require an alternative perspective. You may not even realize that you do. For instance, if you have breast cancer and you talk to traditionally minded women friends and doctors, they're all going to tell you pretty much the same thing. You won't consider talking to someone with a different viewpoint who can present different, maybe lifesaving, options. Your paradigm limits you.

How might you treat others differently?

I know a selfish person who only considers his own needs. His world begins and ends with him.

Long-time friends finally rejected him for being that way. If these people had responded to him differently from the start they might have helped him to see the way he was. They might not have had to wait for a crisis to occur where they rejected him for being selfish. At the very beginning they could have said, "I will not accept you, nor will I share anything with you because I find your actions and attitudes selfish." But instead they ignored his selfishness until it became too much to bear. They blamed him later. That's the way a lot of people are.

How might you change the way you respond to others?

What messages do you tell yourself?

Listen to the messages you tell yourself. These are messages you should pay attention to. Talk them out in your mind and actualize them. If you say, for example, "I know I should be healthier," think about ways to make that happen. Affirm, "I'm going to be healthy," and create a program to change. Change your attitude, your beliefs, and your support system to encourage health. Then you will change the silent voice to an empowering one that helps you to actualize what you want to become.

Change only those attitudes, actions, and beliefs that you don't like

You probably accept a lot of beliefs that you don't like. Identify them and write them down. You may believe, for example, that politics can never change anything. As a result, you become cynical and never put your energy into making change happen.

If you want to live a more positive existence you must acknowledge that change is possible and that your input does make a difference. If, for instance, you decide that you want to become vegetarian, you can start associating with other like-minded people. You can encourage friends who want to become vegetarians to do so by showing them that they can refrain from meat eating and be optimally healthy. By doing so, you'll be developing a small paradigm which in time can become a very powerful one. In the 1960s there were only hundreds of thousands of vegetarians in this country. Today there are twenty million. People influenced each other and caused a positive change to occur. They responded to a vegetarian Mr. America and to great athletes who didn't eat meat. These new models gave them the confidence to change.

It becomes more difficult to change certain attitudes and

actions without the support of friends and family. If your family disagrees with your wanting to become vegetarian, changing is going to be much more difficult. You have to be very self-motivated and confident; only the autonomous person can succeed. With autonomy, you can find the inner strength and support you need to make positive change happen.

Anger can sometimes be a strong motivator for change when channeled constructively. A woman I know just ran the marathon. But three weeks ago, this woman had been about to give up because her family had been opposed to her spending time and energy in training. They'd made her feel guilty about it.

She came to me one day and said she wasn't going to race. I asked her why and she replied that she just couldn't do it. I told her she was right, that she was obviously not emotionally, spiritually, intellectually, or physically able to succeed. Then I told her good-bye. She just stood there and looked at me. I asked her what she wanted from me. I wasn't going to encourage her to do something she didn't feel capable of doing. She said she was physically able to do it and I disagreed. I told her she wasn't or else she would run. I said, "You obviously just can't do it. You tried and failed and it's alright. Now you can go back to being all the things you were. You can gain back your weight and your negative attitude. You can become cynical and bitter and let all your friends and family affect you. That's obviously what you want because that's the choice you've made, and it's okay. Make that choice. Live with it."

She got really angry. And I said, "People sometimes work extremely hard to climb a mountain. They almost reach the top. Just a little further and they would suddenly see every vista that's in front of them—all the unlimited possibilities. But they allow other people and their fears to just drag them right back down again. You came that close."

The next day she called me and said, "I told my family and friends that if they open their mouth to me today I would smack them." She said, "I'm going out and I'm going to stay by myself until I get through this race." And she did. And they were there cheering her on.

Today, she's a hero in their minds and in her own. Voices of uncertainty no longer hold her back. Once you break free and become autonomous you gain inner power. A transformation occurs when you see positive change occur. Your perspectives and attitudes change. Then you notice that people who were against you are now on your side. The same people who denied you support are now looking up to you and even bragging about you. I can assure you that the day of the race the family of the woman who ran the marathon, who did nothing but badger her for months, told everyone they know about her accomplishment. Now she's a paradigm leader. Remember, a paradigm can be as small as your own life or your relationship or your family.

How did your parents treat each other?

Look at the way your parents treated themselves and each other. You learned from them as a child and are now, perhaps, a reflection of who they were. Have you incorporated their qualities—the best and the worst? Identify these qualities so you can change the ones you don't like, keep the ones you do, and, in the process, become more truly yourself.

Do you take responsibility for your attitudes and actions regardless of who is on the receiving end?

How do your attitudes affect other people? Does it feel good being at the other end of what you're sharing? If it doesn't feel good, then change it.

People in positions of power don't usually think this way. If they are "above" someone else, they assume a superior attitude. People with less status aren't given equal respect. All around you see the ritual of inequality. Our society accepts that. You'll be standing in line and a rich and powerful person will walk right by you and get immediate attention.

All this is a facade. An attitude of superiority has no power if you don't acknowledge it, since power is an illusion. It doesn't exist unless you acknowledge it's real. When I counsel a member of a royal family of Europe, which I have, they come to me without their title, just as a person. They'll sit across from me and I'll treat them just like any other person. I don't use titles. I don't call myself doctor and I don't use titles with anyone else. A person is just a person.

Can you imagine how you could communicate with people if you felt you were equal to everyone you met? You would be removing the distance between yourself and others and relating person to person. Respecting people's differences is fine. Respecting their uniqueness is fine. But respecting their so-called superiority is not. In our society, differences are equated with superiority or inferiority. And that has to change.

Define the different systems that you accept or belong to in which you feel inferior. Find those systems or relationships in which your attitudes, beliefs, and actions are always considered of secondary importance to someone else's. Acknowledge that you are equal to every other person. Becoming aware is the first step in changing the process.

Forgiving: Letting Go of Pain

I ASK PEOPLE ATTENDING MY WORKSHOPS ABOUT THE CHALLENGES THEY face in their lives. One person said he feels conflicted about what he really wants. Being conflicted is like saying, for instance, I want intimacy and solitude, or I want to eat healthy food and junk food.

How do you reconcile these? It's simple. You recognize that, at any given moment, every single thought has its opposite in your consciousness and you determine the advantage of each side.

Acknowledge that you have opposing thoughts and desires. Otherwise, you'll bury unwelcome ideas. They'll remain inside of you and are likely to come out later. That's where you harm yourself and others. You may do things and then think, how could I have done that? A part of your nature may emerge that you didn't consciously realize was there.

You will know exactly who you are by understanding what you are capable of doing. Then you can decide how to act in your own best interest. If you're trying to be a happy, wholesome, healthy person you won't entertain the dark thoughts and feelings that are there. Once you get into the habit of making the right choices for yourself it becomes easy. You start to know when you're making the correct decisions.

Of course, being human, you sometimes choose wrong options. That's okay as long as you can recognize what you've done and learn from your mistakes. You'll scream at someone, you'll do something that in retrospect is stupid. And then you'll say, alright, I acknowledge that I made a mistake. What can I do? Forgiving yourself is key to rebalancing.

So is forgiving others.

The whole idea of forgiveness is to allow yourself to go forward. If you don't forgive, you are stuck with the anger and pain of the event. You honor that pain more than your right to go forward without it. All of the love and kindness in you and directed toward you will mean nothing if you're not willing to acknowledge why you're in pain. Forgive the pain and get on with your life.

Who creates your pain?

Although you may blame others for the distress you feel, your pain is your own doing. You create it. If you were to write me an insulting letter, for example, calling me arrogant, conceited, and self-righteous, I could choose to become very angry. I could strike back in an attempt to retaliate or I could go to the other extreme in an attempt to prove how nice I really am. I could internalize what you say and become depressed. With any of these responses, I am causing myself pain by reacting to what you've said.

Another possibility exists. Before reacting, I can take a step back and think about the situation. That way I'm distancing myself from the immediate conflict and putting it into perspective. I can look at the letter you sent and think about your possible intentions. I might decide that I took what you said out of context. Maybe I'm misinterpreting and assuming something that wasn't meant.

If you react to a situation without thinking it through, it's difficult to later change your mind about what happened. Once you become emotional and retaliate, you start justifying your actions. Your ego tells you that what you did was right. Unnecessary conflict arises.

Realize that people have the right to their feelings. Some will like you and some won't. That has nothing to do with you. As long as people don't spread lies to hurt your reputation or physically harm you, they are entitled to their opinions.

When you start to feel distressed, take a step back and ask yourself, what is really happening here? Do I have to accept this situation as painful? Must someone's negative feelings toward me affect how I feel about myself?

List the old hurts you still feel

What old hurts do you still keep alive? Which ones come up over and over? Perhaps some of these sound familiar: Your mother wasn't there when you needed her. You were abused, rejected, ridiculed, or abandoned. Someone stole from you. Something that was supposed to have been given to you was given to someone else.

You must give up old hurts to be free to live more fully. Otherwise, the pain from the past influences the present. You keep yourself from relating to others because you were abused or abandoned earlier in life. You want to be open and trusting, but you have painful memories of being manipulated and taken advantage of. So you hesitate to be yourself. You keep your relationships from working because of the way you were treated previously. That happens when you don't let go of the past.

Living life fully involves taking risks. Unless you take chances, your past fears prevent you from growing.

Examine the hurts that keep reappearing in your life. See what makes you emotionally imbalanced. Notice the patterns. Resolve the hurts and they will stop reappearing. It may seem easier said than done but you are put into painful situations for a reason. There are lessons you need to learn. Work your issues through and in time you will resolve them. You will regain balance if you work at it.

How do you deal with hurt or pain?

Do you hide it? Scream it out to the world? Do you distract yourself? Do you go into therapy? Do you chronically complain and whine? Do you share pain with someone else?

If you deal with pain in any way except by making constructive changes, then you are keeping your hurt alive. Therapy tells you that your hurt is real. While the right kind of therapy has the potential to do you good, sometimes therapy can serve to reinforce your pain, making it more genuine. When this happens, your whole immune system becomes depressed. You start manifesting physical symptoms. The pain grows and becomes as tangible as a tumor and takes on a life of its own.

Therapy can also make you dependent on someone else. You start to feel you can't resolve your own problems. It's disempowering to suggest that unless you're being helped by someone you're incapable of positive change.

I see this often in the recovery movement where people must acknowledge their dysfunction and then go through a program involving several steps. Everybody has to go through the same stages. People are discouraged from dealing with problems on their own, even if they feel capable of doing so.

You may distract yourself from pain by looking for things to take its place, such as food, drugs, or being overly responsible. But a better approach than distraction is to take quiet time every day where you can be introspective. This allows you to face what's bothering you, and put your problems into perspective.

Sometimes you want to share your hurt with others, but after a certain point, this doesn't do any good. I have friends who always want to share their problems with me. This is fine, except when it's the same problem over and over and they never change anything. Then, I simply ask them what they're trying to achieve. Are they talking just because I'm willing to listen? They share the same thing over and over, until I don't want to hear it anymore. Finally I tell them, "If you're not willing to change, don't share your problems with me anymore."

Perhaps most of the pain you now experience is not real but you make it appear real. Is that possible? Be honest. Perhaps much of what you're calling your physical crisis does not exist but is self-created. Is that possible? If it is, remember this: Until you let go of self-created or self-perpetuated pain and no longer treat it as a real problem, it will continue to live.

Intellectually you might understand this but nothing will change until you actually let go of your pain and fill your mind with affirmations to reprogram your body and mind. Tell yourself that you're pure, whole, complete, healthy, positive, lovable, and an ideal human being who deserves all the good things life has to offer. Until you do, the old messages will supersede it.

Once you start believing in yourself completely, you'll be amazed at how far you can go. Where you didn't think you had the resources, your self-confidence will enable you to accomplish what seems impossible.

People ask me how I do all the things I do. I've written fifty books and done 165 television programs. I've produced sixteen documentaries and thirty-five specials. I've built resorts and detox centers and have owned and operated health food stores and natural food restaurants. I have done more than 7,000 broadcasts and helped over 20,000 people race marathons. How do I do it? I've never gotten around to believing that there's something I can't do. I believe that I can do anything. As a result, anything I want to do I just do.

The only person that can stop me is me. The moment I listen to anyone else's doubts I stop myself. People might say, "Gary, you can't do that because you don't have the education, support, or money. You don't have the institutional systems behind you." Maybe I don't, but I don't need those. I don't accept what people say I can't do. In my belief system I make up the rules.

Some people try to stop me. I've been called a quack, a charlatan, and a fraud. Some people even try to make me appear crazy. But there's no way they can convince me that I'm anything other than a perfect human being. As I result, I continue to go forward. I don't waste my life in frivolities and fear. I'm not motivated by what I can't do but rather by what I can. So everything people say can't be done I end up doing.

I believe the human spirit is perfect. As long as I'm in touch with that spirit in my body, mind, and soul, I realize my perfection. I just have to trust enough to connect with it.

At some point you might say, "Gee whiz, if Gary's done all these things then maybe I can too." Of course you can. I'm no more special than anyone else. I wasn't born or raised differently. I have as much dysfunction in my background as most people. But I choose not to identify with that dysfunction. I don't let myself be a victim sitting around feeling sorry for myself. I could be like most people who are in therapy three days a week reinforcing their dysfunctions. But why hold on to that?

This is your journey. There's no other support system you need. You need only you. Look for resources out there to help strengthen you, but don't depend on them.

Now is the time to look at the pain you've held onto and let it go. Reaffirm every single day that you do not need that pain in your life, and give yourself something in its place. Create small goals, intermediate goals, and major goals. Focus on achieving those. Don't let anyone tell you that you can't do anything that you want to do. If anyone else has accomplished something then you can do it too. Recently, there was a news story about an eighty-six-year-old woman who just raced the marathon. She started training at the age of seventy. Who would have believed it? The fact that she did it means that others can too.

Become the hero in your own life. Have the courage to go out there and make changes. You will meet obstacles of course. You have to differentiate real from imagined obstacles and reject the imagined ones.

What do you enjoy?

Notice what you enjoy doing and engage in those activities often. Enjoyable experiences will give you the confidence to continue doing things that are good for you. That's why I've been running marathons for twenty years. It feels good and it reaffirms my right to be strong, disciplined, and integrated in body, mind, and spirit.

Are you happy in your work situation? I never work at a job I don't like. Yet many people feel stuck in their work. They argue that they must stay there; they have no choice. These people justify their actions with questions such as, "Who is going to pay the mortgage?" "Who will feed the kids?" "Who is going to pay the health insurance?" Their concerns go on and on. Thus they rationalize being stuck in an unhappy situation.

Ask yourself, do I enjoy my surroundings? Recently, I visited the southwest to see some old friends. I did a workshop in Santa Fe where I got to talk to some ex-New Yorkers.

I spoke to one woman who is a jewelry designer. She makes costume jewelry and jewelry from platinum, gold, and silver. This woman loves her work and enjoys the pace of life of Santa Fe, the cleanliness, being close to nature, and the people. Most Santa Fe residents will let you be whatever you want to be; the whole community acknowledges freedom of expression.

I also met a third-generation police officer. He told me how difficult it was for him to convince his Irish Catholic family that he wanted to do something else with his life. He does landscape architecture, which he loves. His life is fulfilled. He feels balanced. As a result, he no longer suffers from migraine headaches. He has lost weight. He's happy in his marriage.

These people weren't afraid to make changes. Think of how your life would change if you did things that made you feel good and were around people who supported you. That doesn't mean that what you are doing is not what you should be doing. I'm just suggesting that if you feel trapped you may need to go forward.

If you find yourself unhappy in your living or working environment, take a step back and look at both sides of the issue. Fold a piece of paper in half and on one side write about why you stay put in the same location, the same job, the same lifestyle. Why haven't you let go of your pain, anger, disappointments, and hurt? Why do you continue to blame yourself?

On the other side, list what you would ideally like to do. That way you can focus your attention on it. Write about the resources you will need to achieve what you want to do. Maybe a year or two of schooling is necessary to get the skills, credentials, and support system you need. Your written ideas will give you a plan of action. You'll have goals to focus on.

Selecting a job or a place to live based on what gives you the greatest pleasure may be a difficult concept. Society doesn't teach you to associate happiness with lifestyle. You've been taught that you can only attain so much. You are told you are limited because of your education, class, gender, culture. Your belief system says that what you have is the best that you deserve and the best you should expect.

You have to stretch your beliefs to go beyond that notion. Why should you accept a barren little island as your reality when you've got a whole continent to explore? You probably do so because you've been told that's what you can expect. You're middle class. You come from a certain background. Everyone else does it this way so you've got to do it this way. Your whole life becomes circumscribed by your supposed limitations.

It's easy to lose sight of possibilities that can enhance your life and bring you greater enjoyment. If your family has never gone to the ballet, for instance, you don't go to the ballet. If they have never gone to an art exhibit in Soho, you don't go either. If they've never been hiking, you don't do that either. You don't do anything outside of what is expected.

If you accept the expectations that everyone lays down for you they become as formidable as an impenetrable, unscalable prison wall. These limitations don't really exist, but you make them seem real. Instead of taking a step back to differentiate between what's real and not real, you are prone to staying limited. You'll say things like, "We're in a recession." "I can't change." "The only jobs I can get are jobs I don't like." "I'm stuck in my ways." "I'm too old." "I have to live with it."

Such words justify your lack of motion. Instead of changing you become frustrated and start to sublimate. You indulge in alcohol, food, television, or sex. You find endless ways to distract yourself.

Experiment with new experiences and behaviors you might enjoy. Once you identify what you do enjoy, create a support system with people that enjoy the same things. One of my friends likes to cook and watch movies. So do I. We've watched movies for six hours at a time. His energy is compatible with mine, and we have enough in common to build a friendship. You want to be with people you feel comfortable with, who reinforce a lifestyle that makes you comfortable.

Doing what is natural requires little effort. It feels as though you are doing what you should be doing. Ask yourself, what do you feel good about doing? What do you look forward to? What gives you great joy? Build your life around these things.

What do you gain by letting go and forgiving?

Write down the following: I'm going to forgive _____ because I will gain _____ This exercise allows you to see how you will benefit from giving up the pain and anger connected to your feeling hurt. It shows you there is a reward in giving it up.

Once you can let go and forgive, you can get on with your life and move forward. The more you release, the freer you become. Life is an educational process. With each lesson you learn to live it more constructively. You keep rebalancing yourself.

Decide what you want to change. Then find the strength

and resources to make the conversion, step by step, day by day. Remove something that you don't feel you want and put something that will work in its place.

What have you learned from your pain?

There's a lesson in pain. Pay attention to what it teaches you. Once you learn the lesson you're not going to repeat it. You can share what you've learned with others and help them in the process. The lesson of pain can be learned by examining who first creates the situation which results in a reaction of pain. For example, when you say something without thinking or knowing that it will provoke a reaction in someone; then, when they do react, you feel pain. Another example: you're frustrated, but instead of dealing with the frustration in a constructive way, you overeat something that's bad for you; then, the next day, you feel an inner pain for what you perceive as your weakness in relying on your old, self-destructive behavior patterns.

Remember a difficult time in your life. What did you learn from that experience? How have you grown and become better for it?

If you could be an unbiased mediator in your own conflict, what would you suggest both sides do?

List your major conflicts. Now take the role of arbitrator and assess the pros and cons of both sides of your conflict. Let's say you have a conflict about being married. First note the benefits of being on your own. You are free to make up your own mind. You can live for yourself. You won't be part of a co-dependent relationship. You have time for yourself. You can make mistakes without being criticized. You can create your own schedule instead of working around someone else's. You don't have to wait for someone else's approval before doing things.

The negative part of being on your own might be that you feel incomplete. In our society you're nobody unless you're a part of a relationship. You may feel insecure being alone. You may think you're unlovable and that something is wrong with you. People do not expect you to be happy being single.

Then look at the other side of the issue. What are the benefits of being married? You have the security and companionship of another person, someone to wake up with and grow old with, a person that will share love and affection.

The down side might be going into debt buying things you need to have as a couple. Things may become more important than the relationship. You may go into debt buying a house you don't really like or need. Soon the relationship may exist to pay for the mortgage, the furniture, and the children. The stress will put a damper on the relationship, and it will no longer be joyful.

When you look at everything from the positive and the negative aspects you will clearly pin down what the ideal situation would be for you. Then you can make your move.

What gives you an adrenalin high?

Most people live their whole lives remembering the one or two rushes they experienced early in life when they were willing to take some risks. If you start taking some chances now, you can feel charged all the time. You can become the adventurer in your own life.

Think of times you felt excited to be alive. Perhaps you were going down rapids, starting a romance, beginning a new career, seeing the Grand Canyon, or going down a roller coaster. Find ways of creating new highs for yourself and you will have something to look forward to every day.

Letting Go of Fear

FEAR IS A PRIMARY REASON THAT PEOPLE DON'T PROGRESS. I TALK TO many people who read good self-help books, seek counseling, attend workshops and seminars, and yet remain stuck in their problems. Nothing changes until they break through their fear.

Sometimes fear is justified, but most of the time it is the result of illusion. I'm going to try to differentiate between the two types of fear—real and illusory—and show you several ways of dealing with each. You can approach real fears pragmatically. Illusory fears need to be eliminated from your mind.

(Note: My answers are not the only solutions nor are they necessarily right for you. Rather, I hope they will inspire you to think of answers that are personally meaningful. In addition, my questions should help you generate questions of your own. Some thoughts will appear immediately, whereas others will come to you later.)

This section will help you to explore what you're afraid of and analyze how you manifest your fears. It will encourage you to think about ways of letting fear go so that you can live a more full and vital life.

What are you afraid of?

Many factors can cause fear. See which of the following makes you fearful.

Fear of losing self-esteem

You lose self-esteem when you fail to live up to your image. Athletes who lose a game posture themselves in a humiliating fashion before the public. They don't say to themselves it's just a game. I'm not going to lose any sleep over it. It's not all that important. They take themselves seriously and take losing to heart.

Where in your life do you strive to maintain an image for fear of losing self-esteem? You may feel bad about not getting a promotion, for example, or about not being able to appear responsible.

Fear of being out of control

If you're like most people, you're terrified by the possibility of your life getting out of control. When is the last time you really played? If you're part of the baby boom generation, there's a good chance that the answer is a very long time ago. Does this sound like you? Every minute of the day is purposeful. You work too hard and never have time just to enjoy yourself. You become successful at doing things but not at just being. I meet a lot of people like this. They always feel the need to be responsible and productive. They can't spend the weekend just hanging out and having fun. They always feel the need to be doing something. They're afraid of losing control.

Even their vacations are planned out and timed from beginning to end. They'll go to Cancún and spend a half hour playing tennis, and a half hour scuba diving. An hour after arriving, they're wondering if they could make a deal on a condominium. All their meals are during meetings.

When I go to a resort, I'm nowhere to be found. I'll be on a hammock somewhere resting. I go away to rest. I don't want to do any business. I don't want to think. I just want to relax and play.

Being out of control asserts that you are different and independent and not just like everyone else. Allow yourself to be out of control. Be creative in a way where you do something spontaneous and completely out of character. Let yourself go, and use being out of control as a way of growing.

On a societal level, being out of control can have positive implications. I constantly work to break through barriers in order to make people aware of their alternatives. Five years ago I said on television that AZT was hurting AIDS patients and that alternative therapies were helping people stay alive. I was out of control in the sense that I was saying things that other people wouldn't dare speak about. They were in a controlled situation, but I wasn't. Of course, in the long run, there is no controlling the emergence of the truth.

Most journalists will not risk being out of control. They have too much to lose going against the system. People such as Mike Wallace and Tom Brokaw are bound by fear. They're afraid of losing their jobs and their power, and—as a result of these losses—their self-esteem. Think of what would happen if more people didn't play by the rules. We could progressively move forward as a society. Until enough people break those barriers, fear will keep us trapped.

Fear of loss of place

You may fear losing your place in different areas of life. In a relationship, for example, you become jealous and hurt if your partner tells you that he or she has met someone else. Jealousy has always puzzled me. I've never understood the concept. If I were in a relationship where someone didn't want to be with me anymore, I would feel fine about that. It wouldn't be a problem. I would get on with my life rather than feel hurt and betrayed. I wouldn't compete against anyone or fight for someone. I don't see the point in that. I would just move on.

As a student, you may have feared losing your place in school. People are put under a lot of pressure to perform well in school. Remember the people who were always competing for A's? Their lives were often imbalanced. They had to give up developing other areas of their lives in order to become school-smart. There's a type of person who always strives for goals but neglects the process leading up to their attainment, and this is sad. The person achieves something but learns nothing in doing so; everything gained boils down to a trophy to be displayed, and it's only through the trophies that the self-esteem is manifested. I see this all the time.

Fear of authority

Authorities want to dominate you. They make you feel that you must comply with their demands—or else. In any confrontation with authority, you may feel afraid, and you react by humbling yourself. The IRS sends you a letter and panic sets in, followed by anger and helplessness. How can you fight an institution that has everything on its side? You're just one person. You allow this insensitive, uncaring bureaucracy to affect your life.

Or you get pulled over for a traffic violation. Whether you are guilty or not, you feel helpless and act childlike. You answer the officer's questions obediently and try to act humble instead of standing up for your rights.

Fear that your real needs will not be fulfilled

Most people live unfulfilled lives. They learn early in life that their own needs are unimportant and carry that belief with them into adulthood.

Parents often live through their children instead of helping them discover their own interests and attain things important to them. As a result, children may become ego extensions of their parents' dreams. A high school student becomes a football player because his dad wants him to be an athlete. Perhaps the child wants to be an artist. He is actively discouraged from doing so. His father tells him that is something girls do. The boy's need to explore life through art is supplanted by his father's need for him to become an extension of his ego. Conversely, a child might want to become a football player but not explore that possibility because his parents fear the sport is too brutal and unnecessarily competitive. Once again, the child is acting out of a need to be accepted by his parents.

Most schools distance children from their own interests as well. They program pupils to learn things that have no relevance to their lives. A curriculum board that is out of touch with students dictates what the children are supposed to be learning. Teachers force them to regurgitate facts instead of explore what is interesting and important to them. As a result, the student's natural curiosity is killed early in the game. Children either learn to become school-smart to get good grades, or drop out if they see nothing in it for them. Either way, they are never encouraged to explore and fulfill their own real needs.

So you can grow up with your real needs never being met. You may learn to be a certain kind of person who acts and reacts in certain predetermined ways. But maybe those ways aren't you. Maybe the real you has a different voice. If you are still in touch with your real needs you end up living a surreptitious existence where you keep a real part of yourself hidden from others lest they judge you harshly for it.

Fear of manipulation

You may be fearful of manipulation with good reason. Often, people don't accept you into their lives without wanting you to be a part of their agenda. For example, they're lonely and want you to fill the void.

The best way to avoid being manipulated is to be very aware of how someone makes you feel. Don't just listen to what a person says; look at her or his actions. If a person tells you that she accepts you for who you are but tries to get you to do things that are against your nature, then you're dealing with a manipulator. That person is using you to get something for himself.

Sometimes two people manipulate each other. They overlook the way they are treating one another because they want the relationship to supply them with something else they need, such as good sex or financial security. Two egos are working together but each is working toward its own end. Sooner or later people suffer as a result. Honesty, compassion, decency, and ethics are ultimately more important than the other things you think you need.

A lot of people are in recovery programs where they are acknowledging having been used or having used other people. They are learning to be up front with others and not to be afraid to tell others what kind of person they are. They're learning to say to someone, "This is what I need and expect in a relationship."

Fear of failure

You may be afraid to do something for fear of not doing it correctly. Therefore, you don't even make an attempt. If this describes you, ask yourself, what is the worst that can happen? Consider that most people don't do things perfectly the first, second, or tenth time. That doesn't mean you shouldn't try. It is only through doing that you learn. Keeping something in your head until you can execute it flawlessly will never work. That's not how humans function. Learning is a process that involves practice through doing.

If you were encouraged early on to do things regardless of the outcome, then you probably felt accepted for yourself. You tried things and did the best you could. You probably attempt new things with little anxiety.

Most of us, however, were not so fortunate. As a result, we've become a nation of spectators. We sit on the sidelines and pay good money to watch people who've conquered fear perform. More people would be actively engaged in things if they didn't have to combat the fear of doing them wrong.

Fear of not being in a relationship

So many men and women have suffered in relationships that made them feel trapped. They were living in a war zone, stepping gingerly around emotional minefields. They were scared to say or do anything that might trigger some unwanted reaction. As a result, they would edit their thoughts, feelings, and actions just to keep arguments from erupting. They would do things just to please their partners, regardless of their own desires. They would go to a movie they didn't want to see or entertain people they didn't like. Everything they did was to accommodate the other person.

This happens frequently if you feel a need to be in a relationship, any relationship. You may feel unacceptable being alone. The average man or woman feels that he or she must be married by thirty or thirty-five. Otherwise they worry they'll be considered strange or gay. People may discourage your legitimate right to be by yourself. If you are susceptible to a fear of being unpaired, you may get into a relationship for the wrong reasons and end up feeling trapped.

Fear of speaking up

I know people who keep silent about other people at work who are goofing off, doing bad work, stealing, or lying. They won't say anything because they're afraid of confrontation. Or they're afraid of what people will think, say, or do to them.

Keeping quiet about your point of view hurts you. The situation stays with you when you keep it inside. Part of you knows that you have to have enough courage to stand up and speak out when something is wrong.

A man once walked into my office when I was out. He acted obnoxious and rude to the people there but nobody said anything. When I heard about what had happened I asked why they had kept quiet. They said they didn't want to offend him. He might have been an important businessperson.

The next time this person came to the office I was there. I confronted him and he was shocked. I asked him if he would treat his daughter or his wife this way. Then I said that the people in my office were wives and daughters too. If the only person he was going to treat with respect was me then I couldn't do business with him. I couldn't trust him.

If you're like most people, you keep quiet because of your conditioning. You're taught to keep your mouth shut, to stay in your place, not to rock the boat, not to stand out. You become constrained by fear.

I'm suggesting that you correct or challenge situations as they arise. You can't change everything, of course. You can't make other people change. But you can let them know where you stand. And you can be an example for others. When you stand up suddenly someone else will follow. You will help another person find the courage.

Fear of incompleteness

Do you ever feel as if your life is incomplete? Perhaps you're filled with regret because time has passed you by and you realize that there are certain things you wish you had done differently.

Maybe you thought a relationship would make your life complete. So you devoted most of your time searching for the ideal relationship instead of looking inside and strengthening yourself.

There is no perfect relationship. You have to start a relationship with the self. You need to be a friend to yourself before you can be a friend to anyone else. Love, honesty, patience, and understanding begin with you.

Fear of aging and dying

When you're young, you think you have an unlimited time in which to live. As you get older you accept that you do not have that kind of time. We do have a lot of information now about how to live longer. With what we know we can easily live to ninety healthfully. If you're very disciplined, one hundred or one hundred and ten is possible. That's realistic because the average life span has increased from sixty-eight to seventy-four in just twenty years. We can add another sixteen years to our age span in the next twenty years. Over the next forty years we should add at least another twenty or thirty years to that.

If you're forty, you're not even halfway there. At that point you've gotten your pace and direction. You have greater knowledge, patience, and willpower than you did when you were young. You have developed a lot of skills. Before you had unbounded energy. Now you have sustainable energy. It's like being in the tenth mile of the marathon. That's where you finally feel comfortable. Now you're in your stride. So look at aging from a positive point of view.

You do start to show signs of aging, of course, but there is a lot you can do to slow it down. You start to get wrinkles. Your body starts to lose some of its elasticity. You start to lose your hair. Everyone in my family is bald. I would be too if it weren't for the fact that when I was thirty I began researching what men can do to keep their hair. Now my hair is so thick I have to get it cut once a week. It grows incredibly fast. My hair color is natural and I have no wrinkles. My skin looks younger today than it did twenty years ago.

The idea that we lose strength with age is also misleading. Athletes used to think that after twenty you could no longer be a swimmer. When you were thirty you could no longer be a boxer. At thirty-three you could no longer be a basketball player. At thirty-five you could no longer be a football player. What nonsense. How long you last as an athlete depends upon how well you condition yourself.

I'm an athlete. This year I won Track and Field Master Athlete in the Metropolitan Athletic Congress. I set six American age group records indoors and two outdoors. I won twenty-seven championships just this year, and I beat records that I set ten years ago. And I haven't even reached my peak yet. Why? Because I'm willing to go one step beyond my fear.

If you wake up in the morning with fear, you won't get very far. You may fear you're no longer attractive; that you don't have the same capacity you used to have; that you'll never win competing with people who are twenty.

It's only when you let go of fear that you have control of your day in a constructive way. That control allows you to go forward.

Our parents accepted the inevitability of the aging process. They thought they were old at thirty-five or forty. It was considered normal to eat the wrong foods and to end up with high blood pressure and diabetes. I'll never forget the day my mother decided to cut her hair and change her clothes because she had turned forty. I came home from school and said, "What's going on? Why do you have old people's hair?" She said she was acting her age. She would never think of going out to jog because she didn't want to seem out of place. It wouldn't look right.

When is the last time you saw a senior citizen in a gym pumping iron? Working out can help them to keep their bodies tight. It keeps their buttocks in, their jaws from falling, the wrinkles from appearing, the osteoarthritis and osteoporosis away. But most are not going to do it because of fear of failure.

Fear of the consequences of personal neglect

I was talking with a friend of mine, the owner of a video store. He's gone through a lot of stress and has gained a lot of weight. Now he's having chest pains. I advised him to get the weight off and to deal with his stress. Otherwise, he might end up having a heart attack. He told me he was afraid this might happen. He's angry with himself about it. I said he should use his anger constructively and start taking care of his health. Tomorrow he is going to get a complete physical examination and cardiovascular stress test just to see what's going on.

Until you take care of yourself, you'll have fear and anger. A self-loathing occurs when you neglect yourself. And this applies not just to your physical needs; you must also tend to your emotional, intellectual, and creative needs. You need to stimulate your brain through reading, for example. And you must take care of interpersonal needs. People need to hug, to share, and to love.

How do you manifest fear?

Your fear can emerge in many ways. Do you identify with any of these modes of manifesting fear?

Sickness

Getting sick keeps you from having to face your responsibilities and unpleasant situations. When you're sick, you don't get pressured. People tend to your needs and are kind and accepting.

Complaining and blaming

Whenever I hear someone moan or complain, I know they're reacting from fear. They make excuses for not doing anything. "I'd get out there but it's too hot, too cold, too dry, too wet, too breezy."

Some people are always blaming someone else for their problems. "It's not my fault, it's yours." "You made me sick." "You gave me a headache." People who are always blaming others may think they're getting rid of their responsibilities; actually, they're just manifesting their fear of the responsibility.

Compulsive/addictive behaviors

Fearful people often engage in compulsive and addictive behaviors. They compulsively eat, drink, or gamble, for example. Instead of going out and doing something constructive with their lives, they will engage in acts that hurt themselves. Gamblers who risk everything are in effect saying, I hate myself so much that I'm willing to destroy everything I've accumulated, including the love for my family and my home. I'm going to give it all away because I don't know who in the hell I am and I don't know how to get in touch with my real needs. I'm not happy. If I was, I wouldn't be gambling.

Compulsive/addictive people are wrapped up in their fears. They act in ways that disguise their feelings of terror, as they try to convert their fear into something else.

Escapism

Our society is very escape-oriented. People find creative ways of displacing their real fears. They watch soap operas because they are afraid to confront their own feelings. No matter how bad their problems, they pale in comparison to those of make-believe people.

Chronic tension

A chronically tense person is hypercritical. The intensity is palpable. You never feel relaxed and spontaneous around such a person.

The tense person doesn't always understand why he's on red alert all the time. The fear that is breeding this energy is not apparent. But if you're a chronically tense person, until you get in touch with what underlies that tension and how it affects you, it will limit you.

Notice any unresolved fears that keep you chronically tense. Do you find yourself getting into fights? Are you afraid of losing control, of being less responsible than others expect you to be, or of showing your uncertainty to people? Your tension becomes a symptom of that.

Withdrawing and hiding from your real feelings

When a person hides his or her fear, he's afraid to let others know what he's really feeling. They might criticize him for it. If he's honest with them, they might come down on him like a ton of bricks.

Maybe he had an experience in the past that taught him not to be honest because it was too painful to be. Soon he is dishonest not only with others but with himself, not admitting even to himself that he is fearful. The problem is that now he is living a very limited life. Because of his hidden fear, he's never explored the options available to him.

Describe a life circumstance you would like to change

Ideally, how would you like to respond to fear? Practically, how do you respond?

Think of a situation that you handled inappropriately. Afterward, you probably thought about what you could have said and done differently. You changed the scenario in your mind and came out the hero. You developed an ideal way of handling the situation that was different from the way you actually dealt with it.

Strive for the ideal. I would love to finish the marathon in under two hours. When I'm training I fantasize about having the strength and speed of a gazelle. I acknowledge my practical speed and work from there.

You don't have to live up to your ideal. And don't criticize yourself if you can't reach it; it may be outside of your grasp. But you can at least try for it.

Which attitudes and behaviors do you need to change?

List the attitudes and behaviors that don't work for you. Until you correct them, nothing will change. You will repeat the same old patterns of behavior and continue to manifest the identical problems. If you continue to eat the wrong foods, you will stay overweight. Until you take responsibility for your health, you can continue going to the doctor for vitamin drips and colonics but nothing will really change.

Sit quietly and write about what doesn't work for you. What are you doing that isn't healthy? Are you hurting other people? Are you disrespectful? Perhaps you're a strict parent. You order your children around and discourage them from asserting themselves. You may not even realize how discouraging you are. As a result, your children grow up hating you and probably everybody else. They take on your worst characteristics.

Start looking at your patterns of behavior. Until you do, nothing will change. But once you can clearly see your own behavior patterns, you can then find the courage to change them.

Will you choose loss of control or positive change?

Nothing changes on its own. You have to be the architect of your life in order to direct the change. Otherwise, you lose control and land in fear-provoking situations. If you neglect your health then the doctors and the hospital are in charge. Better to process wellness and maintain your autonomy.

If you become angry at someone for jumping ahead of you in a movie line and start a fist fight, you also lose control.

Now the police, the insurance company, the lawyers, and the judge control your fate.

Think of the times you lost control because you chose not to be the architect of positive change.

Doubting wastes time

Think of a time you wanted to do something but were held back by your doubts and fears. You may be fixated on that scenario and replay it over and over in your mind. You think about what you could have done and how your life would be different. Were your doubts justified?

Doubting can be avoided when you let your intuition guide you. I base every major life decision on intuition. I find that following my feelings helps me to make a right decision, while relying only on my brain often leads me to a wrong one.

Everyone has intuition, but most people in our objectivity-oriented society need to pay more attention to it. When you are involved in a relationship, you know when someone is about to undermine you. You feel it. You know where you fit in. You travel to a country or a town and you just feel right being there. You also know when you don't feel right in a specific place. You know when you're with someone if you feel comfortable or not.

Learn to trust your intuition. Let it be your guide. Pay attention to it and use it. It's an important asset. Once you know what is right for you and act on it, you erase doubts and fears. Then you can go after what you want in life.

Do you validate the positive and invalidate the negative?

Life involves making choices. Each morning, you decide whether your day will be guided by fear or love. If you choose fear you will be interfering with your happiness and growth. If you choose love, you re-empower myself. Your health, for example, is dependent upon your state of mind. Health and disease are processes—not static entities. Your daily thoughts, feelings, and actions affirm well-being or sickness.

You need to get beyond blaming other people, such as your parents, and take responsibility for your life. You can spend your entire life justifying being unfulfilled, or take charge and make your life work. When part of your life is dysfunctional, recognize that you created the pattern and that only you can change it. People play games when they say, I can't do that. They really can. If your life is working in one area, it can be equally positive in another.

Notice negative thoughts and actions and weed them out. It is the weak link in any situation that causes failure. It is what you don't pay attention to that brings you down.

Reclaim your values and emphasize what is important. Identify your real needs. Write down what you need to be happy in your career, at home, and with friends. If you need loyalty then be with people who are loyal friends. If you need honesty in your relationship, don't accept anything less. Break old destructive patterns of behavior. If others can't honor your needs, they shouldn't be in your life.

An example of someone who validated the positive is Dr. Martin Feldman. He graduated from Yale Medical School, magna cum laude. He is a professor of neurology at Mt. Sinai. After all his education he saw that he was not helping his patients and decided to incorporate nutrition into his protocol. As a result, he shifted his practice. But he made a choice. He saw that his methods were not constructive and he changed them so that now they are. He gave up making rationalizations and excuses about why patients weren't getting better. Now he doesn't have to make those rationalizations or excuses.

Don't filter reality

Let reality be what it is. We're always trying to filter what we see and hear to make it into something else. But by seeing reality for what it is, we can deal with it. If there is corruption, we should see it for what it is. Then we can respond to it instead of pretending it isn't there.

Of course it's hard to change the world around us. Sometimes it's impossible. But I've learned that even if I can't change the world, I can change my response to it. I don't have to get crazy, fearful, and angry because other people act that way. I can maintain balance even if others are imbalanced. I can remain peaceful even if others are belligerent. It takes two clashing egos to fight.

I have learned how to remain free of someone else's negativity. I can have negative people around me, but I don't need to be a part of the negativity.

You can learn all these things too.

Starting Over: New Beginnings

Do you ever wish you could go to sleep and wake to find your problems gone? Unfortunately, it's not that simple. Change requires an active role on your part. This section is designed to guide you through change.

You've already decided that you're sick and tired of being sick and tired. Perhaps relationships repeatedly fail. You're stuck in the same old boring job. You desperately want your life to work and are open to a new perspective on living. It's time to start over.

I believe that every person has the capacity to change who he or she is. I do not accept the notions of twelve-step programs, ongoing therapy, and the kind of self-help books that keep you reliving past traumas. You can engage in all these and still stay the same by using the past as an excuse not to actualize the present. You define who you are by what you've done and, in the process, lose sight of your potential.

You need to suspend judgment and become vulnerable in order to accept that there is another way of perceiving life. If you're not open to that possibility then you have no future.

Let's say you act in dysfunctional ways because you were a battered child or your father was an alcoholic, for example. As a child you responded as best you could. As a young person of five or six, you may have had to adapt to an unhealthy situation in order to survive. You didn't yet have the intellectual capacity to deal with these issues. All you understood was that you needed to be loved and accepted.

Many people are influenced by those impressionable years

for the rest of their life. Authority figures, such as superiors at work, may represent your mother or father in your mind. You carefully watch what they do, how they look at you, and what their body language says. You acquiesce to their demands by never speaking up for yourself. When they talk to you, you look down.

Although you appear normal to the world, inside you may be filled with rage. You may sublimate that anger by working compulsively or engaging in other addictive behavior. There are a thousand ways to manifest self-contempt.

Why not change these unproductive patterns of behavior? Don't cling to them your whole life. The key is in acknowledging the present and letting go of the past. Realize that at any moment you can choose between living in the present or in your memories. Let's begin the process by taking an honest look at the following questions. As you reflect on them, see what answers feel right to you.

What are the internal and external limiting factors in your life?

Answering this question helps you prepare for a new beginning. Make a list of your limits. Note the restrictions others place on you, such as those involved in being a woman or a member of a minority group, and those that you impose upon yourself, such as an assumption that you can't learn a particular skill.

Reviewing your list helps you see what restraints you need to overcome. If you hold yourself back because you are a woman, for instance, explore that issue. As a woman you need to know what you're up against. Until recently, women were barred from racing in marathons. Men wanted women to believe that their bodies couldn't handle the physiological stress. The truth is that women are better suited to racing. Today, according to Fred Lebow (director, N.Y.C. Marathon) more women run marathons than men and some women finish ahead of men.

Rampant sexism still prevails throughout society. Some men feel intimidated by women moving into the work force. As a result, male policy makers generally don't offer women the same opportunities or equal pay for identical responsibilities. Most sexual harassment occurs when a man feels threatened by a woman's presence. He suspects that she might be better at the job and replace him. Instead of competing fairly, he demeans her and makes her feel uncomfortable about being there.

Look at your list and ask yourself, where do my limitations come from? Then set your mind on overcoming them. Two dramatic examples come to mind here. The first is provided by a sixty-seven-year-old woman, named Queenie Thompson, who showed up one day a few years ago at my running and walking club in Central Park. She had three elements working against her: She was a woman, African-American, and a senior citizen. During the running clinic, I said to the group that I didn't care how slow anyone was. Today we start a process, I said. Don't expect immediate results; plan long-term goals. I promised them that if they would stick with this and believe in themselves as much as I believed in them, they would reach their goals and become models for others.

We started racing and Queenie was last in a group of a couple of hundred. I thought that everyone was finished when someone told me that one person was still way down the road. I went to meet her. Queenie was just barely moving. She was overweight and had some physical problems. I asked her how she was feeling and she told me that she didn't think racing was going to be for her. Her friends thought her coming to the club was a stupid idea and she should listen to them. She ought to act her age and spend Sunday mornings sitting on the boardwalk with the other old people, discussing her aches and pains.

I asked her then where she wanted to be. She told me she wanted to be here. "I only care where your mind wants to be," I said. "I'm not concerned about your body, because it will improve over time. But you need a strong mind to make the transition possible. Each week, as you get stronger, people are going to become more adamant about your stopping. The better you feel about yourself, the worse they'll feel about themselves. They'll project that onto you. You're holding up a mirror to these people and making them see that they don't have their lives together. You're going to get a lot of negative feedback. If you can handle that, everything else will fall into place."

Queenie kept coming back. For the longest time she was the slowest person there, but she never lost sight of her goal. We kept encouraging her. Sometimes a voice would come into her head telling her to give up and act her age. She learned to pay it no mind. Instead she replaced her limiting thoughts with positive ones. She would say to herself, I'm getting younger. I'm having fun. I'm feeling great.

Her persistence paid off. Queenie Thompson no longer comes in last, but first. She has mounted the podium to take the gold medal for the twenty-third time in three years. Right now, at seventy, Queenie is a world champion. She won two gold medals at the international games. That means she is one of the best athletes, not just in America, but in the whole world.

Queenie Thompson is a completely different person from the woman at that first club meeting. She has a vivacious personality with a positive disposition. Her body is lean and muscular. Her wrinkles have disappeared and she looks like a young person. Her health is dramatically improved as well.

The second illustration is about a friend who overcame limiting beliefs about her work. Brenda Baskin used to be close to 275 pounds. She was very angry and bitter even though she was financially successful as an art director for one of America's largest advertising agencies.

People expected a lot from her and she never let them down. As a result, Brenda had no life outside of work. I'd call her at eight in the morning and she was at her job. At eleven at night she was still there. It wasn't her work she was doing, but work for other people. She often felt uncomfortable but thought she was powerless to change her situation. You can't tell a client you don't want to promote their product because the product's unhealthy. As a result, she became angry.

Finally she decided that she had had enough. She started preparing for a new direction. That took six months. Then she quit her job and went back to school to become a chiropractor.

Now she's a different human being. She lost the excess weight and is light and happy. The child in her is out and playing. She's creating her own art and openly taking care of her own needs. She is becoming the healer she always wanted to be and as a result feels empowered. She understands that this is her life to live, and no one else's.

These are just two examples among many I could give of why I believe there is a champion inside every human being.

Start by setting new limits. See yourself where you want to be. Visualize yourself as successful, as a winner, as crossing the finish line, or practicing a new career, or completing whatever it is you want to do. Forget the rules you've been taught. They're for the conditioned self, not the new you.

Do you consider your problems more important than your ideals?

When you focus on your problems, you never get around to living your ideals. People tell me, "Gary, I'll develop spiritual and emotional growth later. In the future, I'll learn to be loving and nurturing and to develop bonds. I'll get around to doing service for society after I resolve my problems. Then I'll have time to help other human beings."

The trouble is, that time never comes. When you focus on problems, the moment you get rid of one, you replace it with another. You've got to let the problem mentality go.

When your mind is centered on difficulties you tend to compromise your ideals. Notice which problems and concerns you think about. When you need something so badly that you think you can't live without it, ask yourself, what am I giving up? I spoke to a man this morning who told me he resorted to stealing to maintain a lifestyle he and his family are used to living. Of course something is terribly wrong when you lie, cheat, and steal to get money.

I advised him to let his house go. After all, it's just so much square footage. "Your ideals are more important than 1,600 or 2,000 square feet," I said. "You've got a whole world to explore. There are millions of people to relate to and myriad experiences to have. Who says that you've got to spend every ounce of your energy protecting that square footage? Think of how much of your life is wasted guarding that investment. Where is the higher ideal?"

He confided in me that he worried about his family not perceiving him as a provider. To this, I suggested that he and his family become co-providers. In other words, they need to change their priorities and work together. They need to work on their lives, not just be concerned with income. In the process they will experience new people, cultures, and places instead of being prisoners of their own lifestyle. Giving things up can be freeing.

You can't just say, I'll change once I'm free of debt. That never works. The time to focus on your ideals is now.

Fooling ourselves with illusions

Before you can change you need to investigate the illusions under which you living.

Health

Have you been living with our society's common illusion about health? Our paradigm in this country lets people think they are healthy as long as they aren't dying in a hospital. People are never told that disease is a process that takes years to manifest and that they contribute to this process. As a result, the average person doesn't think that he or she has anything to do with creating diseases such as cancer or arthritis. Being passively healthy is a false illusion, and it's one we're not encouraged to challenge.

Could you imagine waking up each day and saying, "I only process wellness." You would allow only healthful foods into your body and positive thoughts into your mind. You would associate only with cheerful people. Well, that's how I live my life. I view every day as a new beginning. I start each morning with a guided visualization in which I tell myself, "This day, the only things coming into my mind are positive, life-affirming thoughts. I assert that nothing but good comes to me and nothing but good comes from me."

Each day I allow nothing into my body that can cause me harm. I had lunch today with some people. As we were eating, one man said to me that nobody can be perfect. Everyone cheats sometimes. I said to him, "It's not a matter of perfection. I never cheat and I don't consider myself special. I think of myself as what should be normal." I continued, "Why would I eat something that is going to hurt me? You may think that you are getting away with something but I know better." I believe that if we make ourselves aware of the effects of our actions, we will never dishonor the body or mind.

You have choices. True self-empowerment means you're using choices to engage in those thoughts and actions that sustain health. Make time each day for intellectual, emotional, and spiritual growth. Honor your heart and spirit. Every day reaffirm a new beginning. Start and end each day looking at your ideal. Don't read headlines or listen to the news. That's negative. It reminds you how bad things are. When you focus on the possibilities, you can let in the new.

Happiness

Many people live under the illusion that they are happy when they are really only complacent. For example, two people who are together a long time may learn to adapt to each other even though the feelings of bliss and excitement are long gone.

Be with people who excite you. I've had many of the same friends for twenty and thirty years, and I'm still excited about being with them. There is joy in our time together.

Love

Love is the most abused word in the vocabulary. People say they are making love when they're not. They're having sex. They say they're falling out of love. In reality, their codependent relationship is ending.

People confuse love with need. They think they're nobody unless somebody loves them because they need someone other than themselves to make them feel worthwhile. People do all kinds of things that compromise their basic values to gain someone else's attention and respect.

In its essence, love is something that comes from inside the self. You need to love yourself first. The more you love yourself, the more love you can give—and receive. You radiate a light that draws people.

Love should be manifested every day, in every way, and it can be. When you're starting over, begin with the idea that you can love yourself unconditionally. Every time you start to get down on yourself, stop and remind yourself that you choose to love yourself.

Job and security

There was, until recently, an illusion that as long as you put in your time and worked without complaining, you would have job security for life. Our society has learned a hard lesson about that illusion in the past decade.

The only way to become secure is to become self-sufficient. Those who wait for someone to take care of them end up disappointed, hostile, and self-abusive. They sit in front of the television set growing fat or chain-smoking. Frequently they abuse their families. They deprive others of their love because their company betrayed them.

These people are terrified of change. They want things to be the way they were told they always would be. They're living by the control and power others have imposed. So when they no longer have a job they have nothing to rely upon because they've never trusted themselves.

You betray yourself by stopping your own growth. As long as you're growing you always land on your feet. You adapt.

Friends

How many of your friends are real friends? Are they there to share something? Or are they there because they want something? Or only *when* they want something? Did you ever think you had real friends only to discover you did not?

Home

People think that they are being cheated out of the American dream if they don't own a home; many perceive owning a home as the most important thing in life. One of the biggest sources of anxiety in America is the fear people have of losing their homes.

In reality, home is your heart. It's where you feel you belong. If we belong to ourselves then wherever we are, we're at home.

Have you been with people or in romances where you didn't care if you had a home? You just loved being with the person. Your whole day was centered around looking forward to what you could share together. Then after awhile maybe you started focusing on the security of a home. The home became more important than the person. No home should ever be more important than love or sharing with another human being.

Make dreams come true

You must trust and believe in yourself. You must get excited by your own dreams and capabilities. Every day I look at the projects that I want to do. Then I write them down. They don't have to be done that day but I want to keep my mind centered on my plans. I get excited by my ideas. I work on one idea at a time. I'm always examining my potential so I can make something happen.

Write down your ideas in order to keep your excitement level up. Put your ideas in front of you every day and just keep working on them. There is no one better than you to be your cheerleader and coach.

What else can you do to make your dreams come true?

Don't welcome your old self back

The moment your old self starts to reappear—you start whining, complaining, moaning, feeling guilty, and feeling bad—stop and say, "Old self, you are not allowed in. Good-bye. Hello again, new self." You've got to keep bringing yourself back to where you want to be.

Don't empower boredom, emptiness, and fear

The moment you entertain fear, you don't try anything new. If you feel empty it is because you are not allowing in all the wonderful things that can fill your life. Think of the beauty of the wilderness, think of how wonderful human nature is when it's honest and open.

Don't allow a moment of your life to be empty. Put joy into each second. You can do this because you have choices. You can choose to spend a moment thinking, I'm not with someone, I'm alone. I'm lonely. Or you can think, I'm going to use this alone time to meditate, to reflect, to work on myself. Then you never have emptiness in your life.

No one who is excited by his or her own capacity is ever bored. How in the world can anyone be bored with the wonderful world we have and all the beautiful people we have in it? There are great places everywhere and amazing things being done by people every day. There's no way you can be bored once you engage in life. You can't engage in one billionth of what there is out there to do. Anyone who is bored is saying, in effect, I'm closing myself off to life. Open yourself up.

Rediscover your childlike aspects

If you're going to engage in new beginnings, this is the most important thing. This is where you get down to what really counts. I believe that in every human being there is a child, and that that child is the most beautiful part of the person's nature. Staying in touch with that part of your nature allows you to be vulnerable and to grow.

Unfortunately, most people learn to tame that part of themselves. First your parents tell you to grow up and act your age. Then your teachers make you sit still and be quiet and obedient. You start to feel guilty and learn to follow their rules and expectations.

To start over in a healthy way, get in touch with the child you've buried inside. Allow the rebirth of that child. Every day find one new quality of childhood and manifest that trait all day. Let it come out at work, during play, and in your relationships. Keep using it. Bring it to the fore.

Look at the following qualities that children often display. Consider how you can use these qualities to enhance your life.

Innocence

As children, we were innocent about everything. As we advance through life, though, we lose touch with our innocence. We abuse the truth again and again, and in time become jaded. We believe the only way of communicating is through deception and half-truths. We let our real needs and feelings be neglected because we don't admit to them.

At this point we need more than ever to re-create the part of childhood that embodies innocence. We need to recall how we once acknowledged the wonder of learning, and how every single discovery was an exhilarating experience that redefined us and our environment. We need to appreciate people for who they are and not judge them by what society and our preconceived notions tell us to think.

By allowing the innocence of our childlike aspect to manifest itself, we are renewing our lives. We can have a fresh perspective once we clean the slate and allow each day to be brand new. Innocence is the quality at the heart of forgiveness and human growth.

Curiosity

Babies have amazing curiosity. Watch a baby monkey, a kitten, a puppy, a lion cub, or a human baby. They all have one thing in common. They find that everything is worth exploring. Every nook and cranny, and everything that moves engages them in exploration. Life is a puzzle that they are actively trying to solve. They want to explore for the sake of exploring; they're not looking for some reward. They will taste things without knowing whether or not they will like them. They have the curiosity to try.

Curiosity allows people to grow. Without curiosity they repeat fixed patterns of behavior and every day becomes the same. I have always wondered how people could not be curious about things like ballet or folk dances, how a fiddle is made, or how a small engine gets a big plane off the ground.

I'm curious about how a heart pumps, how an acorn becomes a tree, and what happens to the spirit after the body dies. All these wonderments stem from a childlike curiosity.

By bringing curiosity back into your life, you renew your passion for living. To do this, you must first eliminate the need for certainty, predictable outcomes, and control over your environment. The need for control smothers curiosity, destroys spontaneity, and extinguishes vitality.

Wouldn't you like to go out and explore people, events, places, experiences? Don't tame your curiosity. That makes you cynical and judgmental. Curiosity allows you to explore and grow.

Energy

If there's one thing that characterizes children, it's energy! If we want to get in better touch with the child within us, perhaps we can attune ourselves to the energy that is everywhere, and tap into it.

There are many forms of energy at work in your body. Electrical energy allows the central nervous system to transmit nerve impulses so that you can move. Chemical energy permits hormones and enzyme systems to synthesize. Thermal energy lets the internal body core temperature stay at ninety-eight degrees no matter how cold or hot your surroundings. Osmotic energy allows lymph and blood to flow through your system. Mechanical energy lets muscle movements occur.

All of these energies are part of a larger system, the life energy, which directs all other energies. Although energy is needed for motion, thought is needed even before that. Therefore, energy is consciousness. I don't tell the trillions of cells in my body what to do. I don't even know all the things they do. Yet they do what they're supposed to do twenty-four hours a day. How is that possible unless there is a grand system focusing all these energies?

Conscious energy always exists. It cannot be created or destroyed. Only its form can be altered. Your life, therefore, is merely a continuum of some energy that is immortal. Your body is a vehicle that, for a period of years, has the opportunity to use the energy you've been given. You may not be the wisest or most saintly person who has ever lived, but you can do something with your life energy if you understand that the first rule of life is to honor it.

By honoring the energy that life represents, you are becoming aware of your connection to nature. You're a part of it, because all energies are connected. George Leonard said that there is a silent thread that weaves its way through all people and connects us.

At some point, you must reconcile the difference between learned consciousness and universal consciousness. What you are conditioned to believe comprises your learned consciousness. That could be wrong. You could learn to be a racist. You could learn that your culture is better or worse than another. You could learn the art of self-denial and avoidance. You could learn insensitivity or subjugation. Then you are living your life as if your beliefs comprise the only reality there is.

It is the vanity and insecurity people feel in their everyday lives that force them to believe that they must continually prove themselves in order to protect what little they have. People constantly struggle to prove that they are worthy of love, respect, or social position. When a person becomes accepted on some level, efficient at doing something, or recognized for something, generally all their time and energy go into maintaining that image.

Universal consciousness, on the other hand, is the ultimate reality. When you connect with it, you intuitively know right from wrong. It permits you to love unconditionally, to respect all life, to honor others no matter what differences exist between you.

You can develop a deeper spiritual awareness by listening to your inner voice. It will connect you to a higher consciousness, which makes you aware that regardless of social position or financial wealth, you are still equal in all respects to any king or sage that has ever lived. The dynamics of a spiritual life balance all other things.

Fortunately, many people have connected to their inner voice and have allowed it to guide them. That's why we have humaneness. That's why we care about suffering, and why we have not lost our empathy and our motivation to be the best we can be.

Capacity to learn

Children learn as naturally as sponges soak up water. Even when we are adults, there is no limit to what we can learn. But we should always remember that learning is not merely the ability to retain and retrieve facts. The most important lessons involve our capacity to surrender the need to be right and allow a natural process of cause and effect to occur. I've seen people who were taught the right way to racewalk and found it cumbersome and mechanically inappropriate for their bodies. When these people were allowed to modify the form so it was less technically correct but better adapted to their own bodies, they did much better. In our society we should begin to realize that our capacity to learn is directly related to our capacity to adjust and adapt to our own unique psychological, emotional, creative, and physiological requirements. No two people are the same. Yet people try to create standards as if all people were alike.

The capacity to learn also means that we can unlearn. The hardest thing to give up is knowledge, especially if that knowledge has served us well in some respects. But what serves us well in certain respects is not always the right thing to hold onto. Much of the knowledge that we have prided ourselves on maintaining is neither useful nor universally true.

A reality should be universal. Kindness, sensitivity, passion, and honesty are universal realities. Yet we alter universal realities to meet our own individual needs. That's not always wise, because we start bringing in our conditioning, which tells us to learn only what will benefit us.

As a result, people don't generally do things unless it gives them an immediate reward, either in terms of recognition, monetary value, or social position. So learning for the joy of learning and for the broadening of our consciousness, and giving up old ideas and replacing them with new ones, are not considered desirable activities.

Tolerance of imperfection

Children don't examine their imperfections. They don't say, "I can't do this because ... I can't do that because ..." They don't particularly care about perfection as a virtue. Adults, on the other hand, like the idea of a flawless work of art, a flawless concerto, or a flawless poem. What is ignored is the process that leads to perfection. What we don't often understand is how many drafts go into writing the poem, how many lessons precede the masterpiece, and how many rehearsals go into the great performance.

I believe that your goal should not be perfection, which is impossible to achieve. Your goal should be, rather, the process that allows you to continue to grow your entire life, and to continue to strive to enhance, renew, broaden, and deepen your awareness of what you're doing, but never to the point at which you feel you are flawless in what you do. That state —flawlessness—should always be just beyond your grasp.

Once we understand that nothing that we do in life will ever be perfect, striving for perfection is no longer our focus. We must continue to stretch beyond our comfort zone, and force our mind, body, and ideas into an area where there are no certainties. It's in the area of uncertainties, where we go further than we ever thought we were capable of going, that new inspiration occurs. Though we don't know how we create it, we do. Answers occur even to questions that we never thought to ask. The process allows that to occur.

Be like a child. Don't look at your flaws. Look at what works.

Fearlessness

Do you ever notice little children acting like little heroes? They're not afraid.

We look up to people who have overcome insurmountable challenges. They become our heroes. And we recognize the struggle of the heroic effort even if the goal is not always achieved. We become inspired by strength and focus in the face of an uncertain outcome. The effort itself is heroic.

Movies are great at capturing the essence of real-life heroism and depicting it for us. In the movie *Chariots of Fire,* the main character, a runner, falls on a track and seems to be out of the race. The film goes into slow motion as he gets back up, so that you can see the agony on his face when he is unsure that he can go forward. Then you see his determination as he pushes himself to catch up to the pack. He must let go of all of his fear, and trust that there is, within him, a strength that he has never tapped. It is that heroic strength that allows him to finally pass the others. In another movie, *Iron Will,* a boy in a dogsled race takes on a 500-mile track that goes from Canada to St. Paul, Minnesota. The boy has to endure everything that can go wrong, yet he never loses his spirit. He never says he's going to stop, even when his body can barely move. At the very end he wins the race with just a second to go, and clearly becomes a hero. People who make such sacrifices and are willing to go through such pain inspire others.

Heroes engage in life. Each day, in their own quiet way, without grandstanding, they go out to push just a little further beyond their comfort zone. That is what strengthens them.

I believe that every person is a hero. You don't have to be a racer or engage in an activity that would be the subject of a movie. But you are a hero when you take a journey to challenge that which seems insurmountable. Start your hero's journey. Find one cause and commit yourself to an ideal.

Honesty

Children have no problem saying what they feel. Most adults lose that ability. Think of what it would be like if you said what you felt. Start doing it. I do. It scares people because they are used to other people telling them what they would like to hear, not what you need to tell them. They want you to edit what you say so they can accept it.

When I do a radio show and tell things as they are, I'm not concerned about whether or not you can handle honesty. I must honor the sanctity of my inner being. You may say, "Gary, I don't like what you're saying. It hurts. I don't want to hear it." Or you may say, "Gary, thank you." The point is, I'm not going to tailor what I say in order to produce only the positive response.

Of course, you have to practice social decorum and be sensitive toward others' feelings. But that doesn't mean you should lie. I'd much rather be with someone who is honest with me than with someone who says what he thinks I want to hear but doesn't mean it.

Wonder

Look at life and be filled with all that is there. Don't restrict yourself to a narrow range with the same repetitive actions and motions each day.

Look for the enchantment of discovery. Have you ever noticed how children do things for the sake of doing them? They don't need to be rewarded; the exploration and discovery are reward enough. A child plays with something, finds it exciting, and then is able to let it go and move on.

Adults tend to engage in activities for the reward. Then, once they get it, they try to guard and control the reward. They accumulate and are afraid of letting things go, because what they accrue becomes part of their identity. They become afraid to let go of their title, success, and money. Adults forget how to explore life for the joy of it. They become prisoners trapped by what they've accumulated.

The person who is happy with life is the person who achieves something but then moves on. That person will also be able to share the fruits of his or her experiences with other people.

Creativity

Children love to create. They create without the need to obtain something from it. You should too.

I write books but I don't allow myself to be called an author. When you call yourself an author you establish an identity. You're an intellectual snob. For me, writing is a creative method of communicating, not a status-generator.

If you create for the joy of it, you become creative in everything you do. You redecorate your apartment, change your work space, or dress differently. Have fun and be creative in all things.

Adaptability

Children will adapt to any environment. You should learn from that. No matter where you find yourself, look for pleasure and joy there.

Forgiveness

Children always forgive. They can't hold a grudge. That's one of their most inspired qualities. Children are able to let go and get on with their lives.

Tomorrow, make a new beginning by forgiving people in your life. Forgive them and let go of the anger.

Happiness

Watch children. They find happiness in little things. In the middle of a wretched environment they still find happiness. As adults we lose that. We may have so much and not appreciate any of it. Sometimes we can't find happiness when we've been given every opportunity to be happy.

Start having happy times and feeling happy. Respect what you do have.

Love and sharing

Every human being has the capacity to love; all of us certainly used that capacity daily as children if given any opportunity at all to do so. I think we should start making a point every day, now, to show love.

The eighties were a time of me, me, me. Everything seemed to be geared to the self. But we're well past that decade. Isn't it time you started sharing with other people? Give something back and share with others.

Trust

A child trusts everyone. Until you hurt a child by betraying her trust, she will trust you. I believe in trust. Until you show me you can't be trusted, I will trust you. I believe trust is essential for growth. You need to trust other cultures, other races, other beliefs, and other religions, and learn from them.

I trust there is good in all things if I look for it. While there is positive and negative in all things, I trust that I can separate the two.

Spontaneity

Children are naturally spontaneous, but as they grow up, people eventually become conditioned to plan everything they do. They start to think, do I want to or not?, about every possible activity.

Why not just do stuff? It will give you freedom. I don't always think about what I do. I just do stuff all the time. For instance, the other night, a friend who had just come from a boring party and was all dressed up, called me. She said, "What do you want to do?" I said, "Let's go down to the Bowery." We did, and as cars pulled up we washed people's windows for about an hour. People would say, "God, that looked like Gary Null!" They'd roll down the window and I'd give them a quarter. I'm sure their analysts are thinking they're absolutely psychotic. "Some guy in a tuxedo washed my window and gave me a quarter." That was fun.

What you remember about a lot of the experiences you share in life are the fun and spontaneity of them. You talk about what is different, interesting, and exciting. Get out of your own way and live.

Ability to dream the impossible

I love it when people tell me what they are dreaming about because they're creating new possibilities. That's exactly what they should be dreaming about.

It doesn't matter if you actually achieve your dreams. The important thing is the idea that you're not afraid of them. You're not scared of what is in your heart. How many times have you chased a rainbow even though you never found the end of it? As a child, I used to run all over the place looking for the end of a rainbow. I'd be gone for a whole afternoon. I'd get lost and not know where I was. I'd ask people, "Do you know where the end of the rainbow is?" I would just keep walking for miles and miles. I never found the end, but it was a wonderful adventure. The adventure was in seeking the dream.

Remember to dream and to follow your aspirations.

Ability to ask for help

When a child can't do something, he or she will come and ask you for help. That seems simple and sensible, but have you ever noticed how rarely adults do that? They won't admit that anything in their life is not working. Ask for help if you need help. There's nothing wrong with that.

Respect for the self

Most people don't realize how worthy they are. Don't victimize yourself; there's no point to it. Be kind to yourself. List your worthy qualities. If you're like most people, you don't focus often enough time on your good points. You have many wonderful qualities. Actually write them down and study the list. Then honor and use your wonderful qualities each day, as a child does.

Stop. Have you played today?

No? Then you're still too serious. Every day should include playtime. You work every day and need play to balance yourself.

A lot of people won't acknowledge their emotional needs. They'll justify not playing by thinking "Adults shouldn't do things like that." It doesn't go with their image. They're supposed to be serious in their enjoyments. They'll think to themselves, I'm supposed to enjoy poetry readings, books, and French movies I don't understand. I'm only supposed to laugh at politically appropriate things.

I believe that every man and woman has a desire to play just as children do. Play is interesting and fun. I want to be around people who are able to acknowledge this part of themselves; I don't want to be around serious people all the time. That's no fun.

Think of the people in your life. Are they able to find time for play, or is the relationship overly serious and predictable? Are you able to play wherever you're at, or do you reserve playtime just for vacations? You've got to be able to play without caring if anyone criticizes you for it.

Stop. Don't bash yourself

Whatever you do is okay. Don't look for perfection. Don't look for everything to be perfect or complete. Whatever you do, it's enough. Pat yourself on the back. Be kind to yourself. You're alright.

Stop. Problems are not about blame

Problems help you learn and grow. We all have problems but unless we look at the solutions we're going to perpetuate our problems. I don't blame anyone for what goes down and what comes around. I simply say, it's a part of life.

Stop listening to what doesn't work

If you're putting your energy in one direction and not finding fulfillment, then change perspectives. Stop asking for advice from the same old tired voices. Get a different opinion. Get your own opinion. Who's life is it? Yours or someone else's?

Seek until you find

You may not know what is right for you in certain areas of
your life. Continue searching for what feels right—no matter
how many efforts you have to make. Don't stop because
you've been conditioned to stop. If it isn't right, then it
doesn't fit. It doesn't mean you or the other person is wrong.
It doesn't mean that the job is wrong. It means that what you
are doing doesn't meet your real needs.

For instance, working at a hundred jobs and quitting each
one is better than working in one place and being unhappy.
I'd much rather have someone say, "Gary, I can't work with
you in this place," than to have the person work for me and
be unhappy about it. If you are honest, there are no hard
feelings. I don't consider that irresponsible. Likewise, I don't
see anything wrong with going out with a hundred people—or
a thousand people—or a million people—rather than settling
for someone who isn't suited to you. Let's face it. With all the
dysfunctional people in this world or functional people who
don't share your energy, you have a right to continue your
search.

How many people do you know who are really fulfilled
with their lives? Very few. But most people compromise their
potential for fulfillment because of self-imposed limitations.

I believe we don't have to make that kind of compromise—
not if we empower ourselves, each day, with the strength to
renew our search.